Celebrating Women's Spirituality

1996

Editor
Claudia L'Amoreaux

The Crossing Press, Inc., Freedom, CA 95019
Copyright ©1995 Printed in Korea

Cover Illustration
Mara Friedman

Cover & Interior Design
Amy Sibiga

Interior Illustrations
Cynthia Cunningham-Baxter

Dedication

Today, Earth's tropical rainforests cover approximately 2% of the Earth's surface. Each year, more than 60 million acres of tropical rainforest are degraded or destroyed—nearly 117 acres every minute.

Old growth covered 15 million acres in the Pacific Northwest at one time. During the last century 12 million acres of this forest have been cleared.

Many of Earth's most ancient cultures worshipped the Goddess in the form of the World Tree, or the Tree of Life. Ellen Evert Hopman in her book, Tree Medicine, Tree Magic, *writes: "The ancient Assyrians and Chaldeans believed that the World Tree was located in the Forest of Eridhu. The Izdubar Epic, found on an ancient tablet, describes the tree as one whose seat was the center of the earth. It is said that it had a root of white crystal and that its foliage was of heaven. They called it The Great Mother."*

I dedicate this 1996 Celebrating Women's Spirituality Calendar to the World Tree—our Great Mother. Blessed Be.

—Claudia L'Amoreaux

1996

January
S	M	T	W	T	F	S
	1	2	3	4	5	6
7	8	9	10	11	12	13
14	15	16	17	18	19	20
21	22	23	24	25	26	27
28	29	30	31			

February
S	M	T	W	T	F	S
				1	2	3
4	5	6	7	8	9	10
11	12	13	14	15	16	17
18	19	20	21	22	23	24
25	26	27	28	29		

March
S	M	T	W	T	F	S
					1	2
3	4	5	6	7	8	9
10	11	12	13	14	15	16
17	18	19	20	21	22	23
24	25	26	27	28	29	30
31						

April
S	M	T	W	T	F	S
	1	2	3	4	5	6
7	8	9	10	11	12	13
14	15	16	17	18	19	20
21	22	23	24	25	26	27
28	29	30				

May
S	M	T	W	T	F	S
			1	2	3	4
5	6	7	8	9	10	11
12	13	14	15	16	17	18
19	20	21	22	23	24	25
26	27	28	29	30	31	

June
S	M	T	W	T	F	S
						1
2	3	4	5	6	7	8
9	10	11	12	13	14	15
16	17	18	19	20	21	22
23	24	25	26	27	28	29
30						

July
S	M	T	W	T	F	S
	1	2	3	4	5	6
7	8	9	10	11	12	13
14	15	16	17	18	19	20
21	22	23	24	25	26	27
28	29	30	31			

August
S	M	T	W	T	F	S
				1	2	3
4	5	6	7	8	9	10
11	12	13	14	15	16	17
18	19	20	21	22	23	24
25	26	27	28	29	30	31

September
S	M	T	W	T	F	S
1	2	3	4	5	6	7
8	9	10	11	12	13	14
15	16	17	18	19	20	21
22	23	24	25	26	27	28
29	30					

October
S	M	T	W	T	F	S
		1	2	3	4	5
6	7	8	9	10	11	12
13	14	15	16	17	18	19
20	21	22	23	24	25	26
27	28	29	30	31		

November
S	M	T	W	T	F	S
					1	2
3	4	5	6	7	8	9
10	11	12	13	14	15	16
17	18	19	20	21	22	23
24	25	26	27	28	29	30

December
S	M	T	W	T	F	S
1	2	3	4	5	6	7
8	9	10	11	12	13	14
15	16	17	18	19	20	21
22	23	24	25	26	27	28
29	30	31				

1997

January
S	M	T	W	T	F	S
			1	2	3	4
5	6	7	8	9	10	11
12	13	14	15	16	17	18
19	20	21	22	23	24	25
26	27	28	29	30	31	

February
S	M	T	W	T	F	S
						1
2	3	4	5	6	7	8
9	10	11	12	13	14	15
16	17	18	19	20	21	22
23	24	25	26	27	28	

March
S	M	T	W	T	F	S
						1
2	3	4	5	6	7	8
9	10	11	12	13	14	15
16	17	18	19	20	21	22
23	24	25	26	27	28	29
30	31					

April
S	M	T	W	T	F	S
		1	2	3	4	5
6	7	8	9	10	11	12
13	14	15	16	17	18	19
20	21	22	23	24	25	26
27	28	29	30			

May
S	M	T	W	T	F	S
				1	2	3
4	5	6	7	8	9	10
11	12	13	14	15	16	17
18	19	20	21	22	23	24
25	26	27	28	29	30	31

June
S	M	T	W	T	F	S
1	2	3	4	5	6	7
8	9	10	11	12	13	14
15	16	17	18	19	20	21
22	23	24	25	26	27	28
29	30					

July
S	M	T	W	T	F	S
		1	2	3	4	5
6	7	8	9	10	11	12
13	14	15	16	17	18	19
20	21	22	23	24	25	26
27	28	29	30	31		

August
S	M	T	W	T	F	S
					1	2
3	4	5	6	7	8	9
10	11	12	13	14	15	16
17	18	19	20	21	22	23
24	25	26	27	28	29	30
31						

September
S	M	T	W	T	F	S
	1	2	3	4	5	6
7	8	9	10	11	12	13
14	15	16	17	18	19	20
21	22	23	24	25	26	27
28	29	30				

October
S	M	T	W	T	F	S
			1	2	3	4
5	6	7	8	9	10	11
12	13	14	15	16	17	18
19	20	21	22	23	24	25
26	27	28	29	30	31	

November
S	M	T	W	T	F	S
						1
2	3	4	5	6	7	8
9	10	11	12	13	14	15
16	17	18	19	20	21	22
23	24	25	26	27	28	29
30						

December
S	M	T	W	T	F	S
	1	2	3	4	5	6
7	8	9	10	11	12	13
14	15	16	17	18	19	20
21	22	23	24	25	26	27
28	29	30	31			

Invocation to goddesses being born

There is a cave deep in the center of your heart.
It is the birth cave of the Goddess.
Do you remember?
You have been there
and your mother and grandmother before you.
Your great great granchildren are there now
and your great great grandmothers and their grandmothers.
Eve is there, and Lilith.
Every goddess that you can name is there,
and those you can't name.
They are chanting the birth chants,
midwifing the future.

Open your ears and hear their words
calling in the goddesses of tomorrow.
Chernobyla,
Goddess of AIDS,
Lady of electromagnetic fields,
of radioactive isotopes,
of solar power,
of dioxin.
Ozona.
Goddess of refugee camps.
Great Goddess of nuclear waste sites, protectress.

Come to us now.
Instruct us in your mysteries.
We need you, visible and pure.
Come to us in our dreams.
Come to us in the menstrual hut.
Come to us in the kitchen.
Come to us on the freeway.

We give you birth.

—*Claudia L'Amoreaux*

World Tree © Rachel Clearfield

January

1 ♊ 6:29p — New Year's Day
Monday

"The world-tree is blossoming."
—*Hildegard of Bingen*

2
Tuesday

3
Wednesday

4 ♋ 6:56a
Thursday

5 ○
Friday

6 ♌ 7:30p — Feast of Koré (Greece)
Saturday

7
Sunday

January

S	M	T	W	T	F	S
	1	2	3	4	5	6
7	8	9	10	11	12	13
14	15	16	17	18	19	20
21	22	23	24	25	26	27
28	29	30	31			

February

S	M	T	W	T	F	S
				1	2	3
4	5	6	7	8	9	10
11	12	13	14	15	16	17
18	19	20	21	22	23	24
25	26	27	28	29		

Woman Trying to Catch the Moon in a Pot © Lisa Cowden

January

8
Monday

9 ♍ 7:29a
Tuesday

10
Wednesday

11 ♎ 5:55p
Thursday

12
Friday

13 ☽
Saturday

14 ♏ 1:30a
Sunday

You say I am mysterious
Let me explain myself
In a land of oranges
I am faithful to apples.
—*Elsa Gidlow*

January

S	M	T	W	T	F	S
	1	2	3	4	5	6
7	8	9	10	11	12	13
14	15	16	17	18	19	20
21	22	23	24	25	26	27
28	29	30	31			

February

S	M	T	W	T	F	S
				1	2	3
4	5	6	7	8	9	10
11	12	13	14	15	16	17
18	19	20	21	22	23	24
25	26	27	28	29		

Sacred Space © Melissa Harris

January

15
Monday — Martin Luther King Jr.'s Birthday Obsvd.

16 ♐ 5:25a
Tuesday

17
Wednesday

18 ♑ 6:07a
Thursday

Mary's wedding Anniversary

19
Friday

20 ♒ 5:15a ☉ > ♒ 10:53a ●
Saturday

21
Sunday — 1st Day of Ramadan

> You wear her livery
>
> Shining with gold,
> you, too, Hecate,
> Queen of Night,
> hand-maid to Aphrodite
> —*Sappho*
> *translation by*
> *Mary Barnard*

January

S	M	T	W	T	F	S
	1	2	3	4	5	6
7	8	9	10	11	12	13
14	15	16	17	18	19	20
21	22	23	24	25	26	27
28	29	30	31			

February

S	M	T	W	T	F	S
				1	2	3
4	5	6	7	8	9	10
11	12	13	14	15	16	17
18	19	20	21	22	23	24
25	26	27	28	29		

Seven Year Old Witch

Start with a rusty, white-speckled
 spaghetti cauldron,
rescued from the roadside on your blue
 banana-seat birthday bike.
In it mix pokeberries, acorns, and milkpod
 fairy silk.
Add several spoonfuls of oak leaves
and a yellow pail of rainwater
with a little bit of beach sand left
 in the bottom.
Let sit in the sun for two Saturdays
on a quartz-flecked boulder
taller than you are.
Then stir with a broom handle
while wearing your great grandmother's
 smart black cocktail dress
hitched up by a scarf in your mom's
 favorite color.
The hem should be muddy from dragging
 around the woods.
Pine pitch in your hair adds to the magic.
Sing an Irish song that your grampa sang to
 your dad,
repeating the sad part three times.
Close your eyes and call out your wish as
 loudly as you can.
Wait.
It will come true.

—*Jennifer Marie Murphy*

January

22 ♓ 5:02a
Monday

23
Tuesday

---

24 ♈ 7:36a
Wednesday

25
Thursday

---

26 ♉ 2:16p
Friday

---

27 ◐
Saturday

28
Sunday

January

S	M	T	W	T	F	S
	1	2	3	4	5	6
7	8	9	10	11	12	13
14	15	16	17	18	19	20
21	22	23	24	25	26	27
28	29	30	31			

February

S	M	T	W	T	F	S
				1	2	3
4	5	6	7	8	9	10
11	12	13	14	15	16	17
18	19	20	21	22	23	24
25	26	27	28	29		

Second Initiation: The Peacock
© Diana Vandenberg

January & February

29 ♊ 0:42a
Monday

30
Tuesday

31 ♋ 1:10p
Wednesday

1
Thursday

2 Imbolg
Friday
[illegible]

3 ♌ 1:46a
Saturday
Shopping w/Mary
Melissa's b-ball game

4 ○
Sunday

As I claim all of the universe within me, I recognize my communion with all of creation. And as I take my place as one among many in that majestic story, I know that I belong.

—*Anne Hillman*

February

S	M	T	W	T	F	S
				1	2	3
4	5	6	7	8	9	10
11	12	13	14	15	16	17
18	19	20	21	22	23	24
25	26	27	28	29		

March

S	M	T	W	T	F	S
					1	2
3	4	5	6	7	8	9
10	11	12	13	14	15	16
17	18	19	20	21	22	23
24	25	26	27	28	29	30
31						

Ancestor

Yesterday I walked across the stones of Wander Creek, listening to the rapids under the overhanging cedar bows. This is a place I love, a place I have walked many times.

I stopped in front of an old cedar stump, logged one hundred years ago from the banks of this creek. Now she is a giant, red, decaying mother 12 feet across. New trees send their roots like snakes pushing down through her stump body into earth. For a moment I felt her full height still, saw her towering in the sky in front of me, felt her roots in my legs, deep and strong. She was so beautiful.

Then an impulse ran through me as if she said—"You think I am old..." With it, I turned and saw in the creek bed, veiled by cedar boughs, a rock that was different from the others. I parted the boughs of cedar and entered a place the earth, the cedar and the waters had shaped as special. Running under the bank and out again into a sheltered rapid pool, the waters sang.

In front of the rock, pure sand formed an island, a beach untouched. But the rock —the rock was a log, an ancient tree mother turned to stone. How old was she? From what ancient tropical forest? A tree I cannot name that grew once, here, before even the mountain was born.

I felt with my hands the cold rock grain, the weight too heavy to move, and I sat there with this ancient ancestor, afraid to even imagine how deeply *her* roots go.

Remembering the Elders

1. Sketch a tree that represents your life tree. In the roots put the names of the elders who have supported and given strength to your life. Try two drawings, one to see "foremothers"; the other "forefathers" (remember that these are not necessarily "blood relatives"). Consider the possibility of a photo collage.

2. Under the branches place the names of those whom your tree of life shelters and nourishes.

—Gwendolyn Endicott

February

5 ♍ 1:22p GRE prep-course begins
Monday

6 Waitangi Day (New Zealand)
Tuesday

7 ♎ 11:30p
Wednesday

8
Thursday

9
Friday

10 ♏ 7:35a
Saturday

11
Sunday

February

S	M	T	W	T	F	S
				1	2	3
4	5	6	7	8	9	10
11	12	13	14	15	16	17
18	19	20	21	22	23	24
25	26	27	28	29		

March

S	M	T	W	T	F	S
					1	2
3	4	5	6	7	8	9
10	11	12	13	14	15	16
17	18	19	20	21	22	23
24	25	26	27	28	29	30
31						

To Make a Talisman

Fold within you
Golden sun;
Wrap around you
Silver moon;
Cloak yourself
In whispering winds;
Root yourself
In the dreams of earth;
Feel within you
The mother-sea;
Feed yourself
With the fires of joy
And know that you
Will blessed be.

—*Noel-Anne Brennan*

February

12 ♐ 12:58p ◑
Monday

13
Tuesday

14 ♑ 3:29p   Valentine's Day
Wednesday

15
Thursday

16 ♒ 2:00p
Friday

17
Saturday

18 ♓ 4:09p ●
Sunday

February

S	M	T	W	T	F	S
				1	2	3
4	5	6	7	8	9	10
11	12	13	14	15	16	17
18	19	20	21	22	23	24
25	26	27	28	29		

March

S	M	T	W	T	F	S
					1	2
3	4	5	6	7	8	9
10	11	12	13	14	15	16
17	18	19	20	21	22	23
24	25	26	27	28	29	30
31						

I am a brown-eyed one

When was the last time you looked into your own eyes, deeply?

An infinity of goddesses waits there to be known.

Wolf, deer, fox, bear, ocelot can be seen if you are patient and keen.

Ancestors greet you in cheekbone and chin (a certain grin).

I am a brown-eyed one,
Goddess of Now.
I meet myself by candlelight, in a mirror my mother gave me.
She is a brown-eyed one too.

What are you?

—*Claudia L'Amoreaux*

February

19 ☉ > ♓ 1:01a   President's Day
Monday   Chinese New Year, Year of the Rat

20 ♈ 5:58p   Mardi Gras
Tuesday

21
Wednesday

22 ♉ 11:08p
Thursday

23
Friday

24
Saturday

25 ♊ 8:14a ◐
Sunday

February

S	M	T	W	T	F	S
				1	2	3
4	5	6	7	8	9	10
11	12	13	14	15	16	17
18	19	20	21	22	23	24
25	26	27	28	29		

March

S	M	T	W	T	F	S
					1	2
3	4	5	6	7	8	9
10	11	12	13	14	15	16
17	18	19	20	21	22	23
24	25	26	27	28	29	30
31						

Guardians © Hue Walker

February & March

26
Monday

27 ♋ 8:10p
Tuesday

28
Wednesday

29
Thursday

1 ♌ 8:47a
Friday

2
Saturday

3 ♍ 8:13p
Sunday

Air, fire, water, and earth are the elemental exchanges linking foxglove to bee, starlight to diamond, compost to soil.
—*Rowena Pattee Kryder*

March

S	M	T	W	T	F	S
					1	2
3	4	5	6	7	8	9
10	11	12	13	14	15	16
17	18	19	20	21	22	23
24	25	26	27	28	29	30
31						

April

S	M	T	W	T	F	S
	1	2	3	4	5	6
7	8	9	10	11	12	13
14	15	16	17	18	19	20
21	22	23	24	25	26	27
28	29	30				

Where I grew up in the northwoods, the old women sometimes came around to re-baptize the infants. They felt that certain priests had left out important parts of the "entry" ritual, that is, the assisting of the soul to take up permanent residence in the physical body of the infant at approximately six weeks of age. Among other rituals the women practiced was the placing of salt in the infant's mouth "to awaken the tongue so that it could be able to say, all throughout one's life, from whence one's soul had come."

They anointed the ears and eyelids of the child with poppy-seed oil so that the precious sight and hearing "of the heavens from which one came" would remain impressed in the child's memory. It was recognized by these old women, who were *the* matriarchs of spiritual life, that a child is born with the qualities of inner hearing, inner seeing, as well as the gift of speaking in a way that is not only linear, but also what they called *mystical*. They felt strongly that if these gifts of inner apperception were not properly sheltered at the onset, and throughout one's childhood, they would be lost, and that the person, and the community of that person, would be much the poorer for it.

—*Clarissa Pinkola Estés*

March

4
Monday

5 ○ Purim
Tuesday

6 ♎ 5:40a
Wednesday

7
Thursday

8 ♏ 1:05p   International Women's Day
Friday

9
Saturday

10 ♐ 6:32p   *leave for Cancun*
Sunday

March

S	M	T	W	T	F	S
					1	2
3	4	5	6	7	8	9
10	11	12	13	14	15	16
17	18	19	20	21	22	23
24	25	26	27	28	29	30
31						

April

S	M	T	W	T	F	S
	1	2	3	4	5	6
7	8	9	10	11	12	13
14	15	16	17	18	19	20
21	22	23	24	25	26	27
28	29	30				

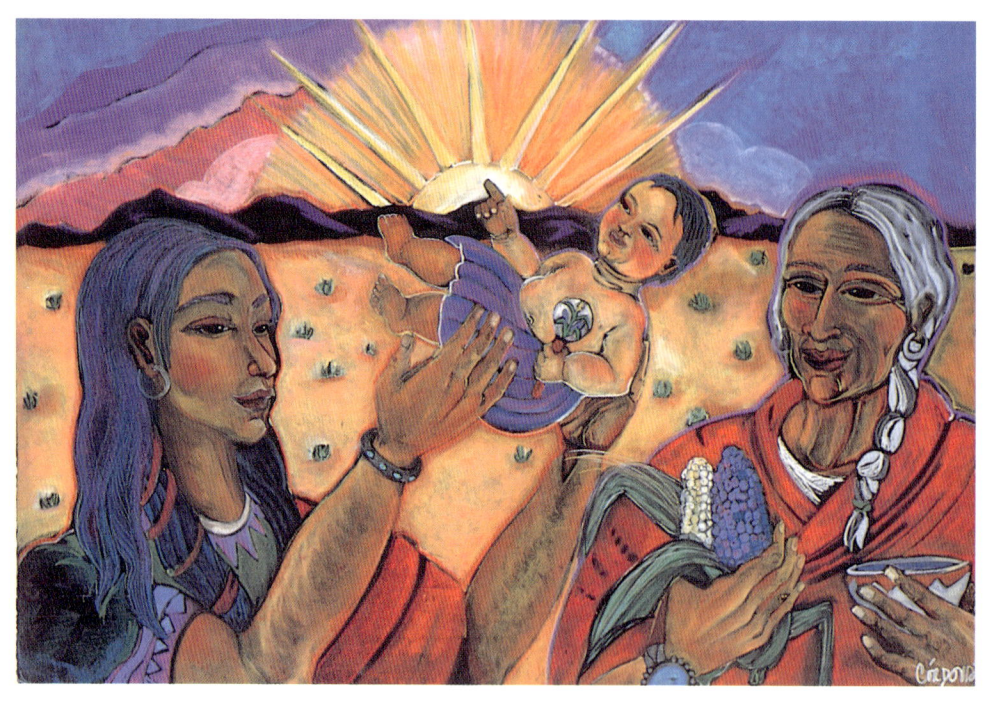

La Tocaya—The Namesake © Amy Córdova

March

11 Monday
Commonwealth Day (Canada)

12 Tuesday
♑ 10:08p ☽

13 Wednesday

14 Thursday

15 Friday
♒ 12:15a

16 Saturday

17 Sunday
♓ 1:50a

return from Cancun

Praise and Love to the Mothers of the World. Praise and Love to the Sisters of the World. Praise and Love to the Women of the World. Praise and Love to my daughters.

—*Luisah Teish*
from an original praise poem for Yemonja

March

S	M	T	W	T	F	S
					1	2
3	4	5	6	7	8	9
10	11	12	13	14	15	16
17	18	19	20	21	22	23
24	25	26	27	28	29	30
31						

April

S	M	T	W	T	F	S
	1	2	3	4	5	6
7	8	9	10	11	12	13
14	15	16	17	18	19	20
21	22	23	24	25	26	27
28	29	30				

Prayer for my daughter Zohara, turning 17

You hurried here from the star realms
   to catch the birth of spring
and the earth was glad to receive
   a being so true of spirit.

Now you stand midwife to a new millennium.
Strong, capable, bold.

In your heart is
   the taste of pure water
   smell of clean mountain air
   power to nurture plants
   courage to protect animals
   wisdom to seek equality
   freedom's joy
   laughter's healing.

In your mind
   the search towards beauty beckons
   and the play of paradox whirls.
In your body dwells
   the love of your own sweet dance.

Listen.
Angels from the future whisper in your ear.
They're singing your song.

The ancestors stretch in your bones,
urging you to your dreams.

The Goddess kisses your hand.

                            —Claudia L'Amoreaux

March

18
Monday

19 ♈ 4:15a ●
Tuesday

20 ☉ > ♈ 12:03a   Spring Equinox
Wednesday

21 ♉ 8:59a
Thursday

22
Friday

23 ♊ 4:59p
Saturday

24
Sunday

March

S	M	T	W	T	F	S
					1	2
3	4	5	6	7	8	9
10	11	12	13	14	15	16
17	18	19	20	21	22	23
24	25	26	27	28	29	30
31						

April

S	M	T	W	T	F	S
	1	2	3	4	5	6
7	8	9	10	11	12	13
14	15	16	17	18	19	20
21	22	23	24	25	26	27
28	29	30				

Thiara's Dreamhorse © Marianna Rydvald

March

25
Monday

26 ♋ 4:06a ☽
Tuesday

27
Wednesday

28 ♌ 4:37p
Thursday

29
Friday

30
Saturday

31 ♍ 4:14a — Palm Sunday
Sunday

"May you live,
 May you flourish
 Like apple-trees,
 Like pear-trees
  in springtime,
 Like wealthy autumn,
 Of all things plentiful."
 —*Roumanian blessing*
  In loving memory
   of Helen Farias

March

S	M	T	W	T	F	S
					1	2
3	4	5	6	7	8	9
10	11	12	13	14	15	16
17	18	19	20	21	22	23
24	25	26	27	28	29	30
31						

April

S	M	T	W	T	F	S
	1	2	3	4	5	6
7	8	9	10	11	12	13
14	15	16	17	18	19	20
21	22	23	24	25	26	27
28	29	30				

Aphrodite © Ruth Zachary

April

1 Monday
April Fool's Day

2 Tuesday
♎ 1:26p

3 Wednesday
○   Daylight Savings Time begins

4 Thursday
♏ 7:57p   1st Day of Passover (Pesach)

5 Friday
Festival of Kwan Yin (China/Japan)
Good Friday

6 Saturday

7 Sunday
♐ 12:21a   Easter Sunday

I have met her
That one
Who holds a true
   divining rod
That one who is
   seeking pure water.
—*Emily Brown*

April

S	M	T	W	T	F	S
	1	2	3	4	5	6
7	8	9	10	11	12	13
14	15	16	17	18	19	20
21	22	23	24	25	26	27
28	29	30				

May

S	M	T	W	T	F	S
			1	2	3	4
5	6	7	8	9	10	11
12	13	14	15	16	17	18
19	20	21	22	23	24	25
26	27	28	29	30	31	

Dance for Spring Saplings © Jane Evershed

April

8
Monday

9 ♑ 4:30a
Tuesday

10 ☽
Wednesday

11 ♒ 7:09a
Thursday

12
Friday

13 ♓ 10:00a
Saturday

(GRE circled)

14
Sunday

We need to stretch out our arms wide to the universe and say:
  "THIS IS OUR BODY."
  —Anne Hillman

April

S	M	T	W	T	F	S
	1	2	3	4	5	6
7	8	9	10	11	12	13
14	15	16	17	18	19	20
21	22	23	24	25	26	27
28	29	30				

May

S	M	T	W	T	F	S
			1	2	3	4
5	6	7	8	9	10	11
12	13	14	15	16	17	18
19	20	21	22	23	24	25
26	27	28	29	30	31	

Meditation for a Good Lunch

Wake up on the *right* side of the bed, with compassion and forgiveness for yourself and others.

Tune in with the outside ... weather, wind, clouds, vibrations. Tune in with the inside ... energy, emotions, body, mind, spirit. Sit in silence, no matter how short. Breathe.

Brew your beverage of choice and eat something light that is grounding and delicious.

Help something grow ... water a plant, feed a cat, nurture a child. Let your creative juices flow —whatever it takes!

... write a poem about your dreams, draw a scene out the window, sing along with an opera, put on drum music and dance ... *Keep* your creative juices flowing, no matter how boring, repetitive or linear the work you pursue.

Stretch your legs, neck, mouth, eyeballs and everything else periodically. Make faces at yourself in the mirror.

Focus intensely on something you care about.

If you keep a list, cross something off of it.

Make and receive phone calls with a spirit of adventure—open to receive a new friend or contact, a problem solved, a challenge discovered.

Pay attention to where you are.

Check outdoors regularly for changes in temperature, precipitation, cloud formations.

When the time is right, prepare a meal of elegant simplicity, (or a succulent feast).

Use the finest, freshest ingredients (or cherished leftovers). Add a variety of texture (more fun and interesting) and a good measure of color (green being a perennial favorite).

Tantalize the taste buds—don't get hung up on salty and sweet ... experiment with sour and bitter.

Enjoy the process. Sing, chant, listen to great music. Breathe. Visualize nourishment in every chop and stir.

Create your eating space—weather appealing, eat outside.

Consider a companion—a friend you invited days ago, or on impulse just this morning ... someone who appreciates your true nature, who'll add a strong dash of laughter to the menu ... (digestion improves when the heart is joyous.)

Or enjoy your own company—have a stream of consciousness conversation with yourself, listen to bird songs, watch plants grow, empty your mind, fill your senses.

Take an inbreath, an outbreath.

Drop unnecessary baggage.

Say Grace. Be Grace.

Remember who you really are.

Chew slowly and mindfully, with compassion and gratitude for the entities that gave of themselves.

Eat with relish and delight.

Have a delicious afternoon for dessert. You know how.

—*Marigold Fine*

April

15 ♈ 1:42p
Monday

16
Tuesday

17 ♉ 7:05p ●
Wednesday

18
Thursday

19 ☉ > ♉ 12:10p
Friday

20 ♊ 2:54a
Saturday

21
Sunday

April

S	M	T	W	T	F	S
		1	2	3	4	5	6
7	8	9	10	11	12	13
14	15	16	17	18	19	20
21	22	23	24	25	26	27
28	29	30				

May

S	M	T	W	T	F	S
			1	2	3	4
5	6	7	8	9	10	11
12	13	14	15	16	17	18
19	20	21	22	23	24	25
26	27	28	29	30	31	

The Lesson #1 © Megaera

April

22 ☿ 1:25p   Earth Day
Monday

23
Tuesday

24
Wednesday

25 ♌ 1:44a ☽   Anzac Day (New Zealand)
Thursday

26   Arbor Day
Friday

27 ♍ 1:49p
Saturday

28
Sunday

> It cannot be gained by
>   gaining it,
> cannot be held by
>   holding it,
> cannot be had by
>   having it,
> cannot be got by
>   going there.
> —*Clarissa Pinkola Estés*

April

S	M	T	W	T	F	S
	1	2	3	4	5	6
7	8	9	10	11	12	13
14	15	16	17	18	19	20
21	22	23	24	25	26	27
28	29	30				

May

S	M	T	W	T	F	S
			1	2	3	4
5	6	7	8	9	10	11
12	13	14	15	16	17	18
19	20	21	22	23	24	25
26	27	28	29	30	31	

*i*f there is a river
more beautiful than this
bright as the blood
red edge of the moon   if

there is a river
more faithful than this
returning each month
to the same delta   if there

is a river
braver than this
coming and coming in a surge
of passion, of pain   if there
    is

a river
more ancient than this
daughter of eve
mother of cain and
    abel   if there is in

the universe such a river   if
there is some where water
more powerful that this wild
water
pray that it flows also
through animals
beautiful and faithful
    and ancient
and female and brave

                —*Lucille Clifton*

April & May

29 ♎ 11:27p
Monday

30
Tuesday

1   May Day
Wednesday

2 ♏ 5:42a
Thursday

3 ○
Friday

4 ♐ 9:05a   Festival of Sheila Na Gig (Ireland)
Saturday

5
Sunday

May

S	M	T	W	T	F	S
				1	2	3	4
5	6	7	8	9	10	11
12	13	14	15	16	17	18
19	20	21	22	23	24	25
26	27	28	29	30	31	

June

S	M	T	W	T	F	S
						1
2	3	4	5	6	7	8
9	10	11	12	13	14	15
16	17	18	19	20	21	22
23	24	25	26	27	28	29
30						

Eve © Colette Crutcher

May

6 ♑ 10:54a
Monday

7
Tuesday

8 ♒ 12:39p
Wednesday

9 ◑
Thursday

10 ♓ 3:29p
Friday

11
Saturday

12 ♈ 8:00p
Sunday
Mother's Day

In the beginning,
people prayed to
the Creatress of Life,
the Mistress of Heaven.
At the very dawn
of religion,
God was a woman.
Do you remember?
—Merlin Stone

May

S	M	T	W	T	F	S
			1	2	3	4
5	6	7	8	9	10	11
12	13	14	15	16	17	18
19	20	21	22	23	24	25
26	27	28	29	30	31	

June

S	M	T	W	T	F	S
						1
2	3	4	5	6	7	8
9	10	11	12	13	14	15
16	17	18	19	20	21	22
23	24	25	26	27	28	29
30						

Befriending the Snake

Plant your feet firmly on the earth. Close your eyes, and breathe. Throughout this meditation, keep your knees soft and flexible. Gently sway back and forth. Feel your entire spinal column. Try to visualize it as a snake. Move your head around, and feel the smooth movement of a snake's head, the alertness of its senses. Imagine that your eyes are located on the sides of your head, near your temples. Sway slowly, like a snake mesmerized by the melody of a flute. For now, let your arms simply hang by your sides, relaxed, only your spine moving, your neck, your head. Nothing else.

The serpent is a creature of the earth. As you breathe, be aware of your feet contacting the ground. Inhaling, invite the earth's energy to enter your spine at its very base. Let your tailbone feel its connection with the earth. As you begin, your spine may feel like a cold snake, a snake with a still, stiff, slow body. With every breath you take, send a gentle wave of movement through it.

There is energy within your spine, and the more you focus on it, and breathe through it, the more it will expand. As it increases, it will want to move. It moves in its own way, guided by a wisdom inaccessible to your conscious mind. You need not control it, or make it move. Your task is merely to remember your breath, and to surrender. Let the snake begin to show you where it wants to stretch, where it wants to contract. Every part of a snake moves, and every part of your own spine can move, from the tailbone to the base of your skull. Enjoy its sensuality, its sure knowledge of where pleasure is to be found.

Feel your entire spinal column, from the base all the way to the top of your head, as a single unit. Nothing moves independently in a snake. A wave of motion that begins at its tail flows through all the way to its head. Let the snake begin to dance with the energy you are sending through it. Call upon it, invite it, talk to it, sing to it. Ask it to awaken in you, to dance through you. Let your spine become warm and fluid like a snake that has been lying on hot rocks, on the sun-drenched earth.

And once your spine is warm, begin to include your entire body in the dance. See if the waves you have generated in your spine want to radiate out through the rest of your body. Waves might start at the top of your head and flow through to your tailbone, or they may flow from the tailbone upward. They may start in your heart and flow out your fingertips. Keep your knees soft, and keep breathing. Move with the gentleness of water.

Look deeply within your body and sense the energy enveloping your spinal column and flowing through the spine itself—a streaming through your very center. Sometimes that streaming needs to free itself through shivering, shaking, trembling. A sloughing off of old tensions and fear. Give in to that trembling should it arise. Surrender to it, breathing deeply, just moving through it. Offer no resistance. Let go of any attempt to control or understand what your body is doing. The serpent has its own wisdom, of which your conscious mind knows nothing.

All around you, energy is flowing, vibrating, pulsating, and all these pulsations are affecting your body. Let the dance unfold, trusting in its perfection. The dance of the serpent is a dance of healing, of moving into at-oneness with all that is.

—*Jalaja Bonheim*

May

13
Monday

14
Tuesday

15 ♉ 2:24a
Wednesday

16
Thursday

17 ♊ 10:48a ●
Friday

18 Islamic New Year
Saturday

19 ♋ 9:16p
Sunday

May

S	M	T	W	T	F	S
			1	2	3	4
5	6	7	8	9	10	11
12	13	14	15	16	17	18
19	20	21	22	23	24	25
26	27	28	29	30	31	

June

S	M	T	W	T	F	S
						1
2	3	4	5	6	7	8
9	10	11	12	13	14	15
16	17	18	19	20	21	22
23	24	25	26	27	28	29
30						

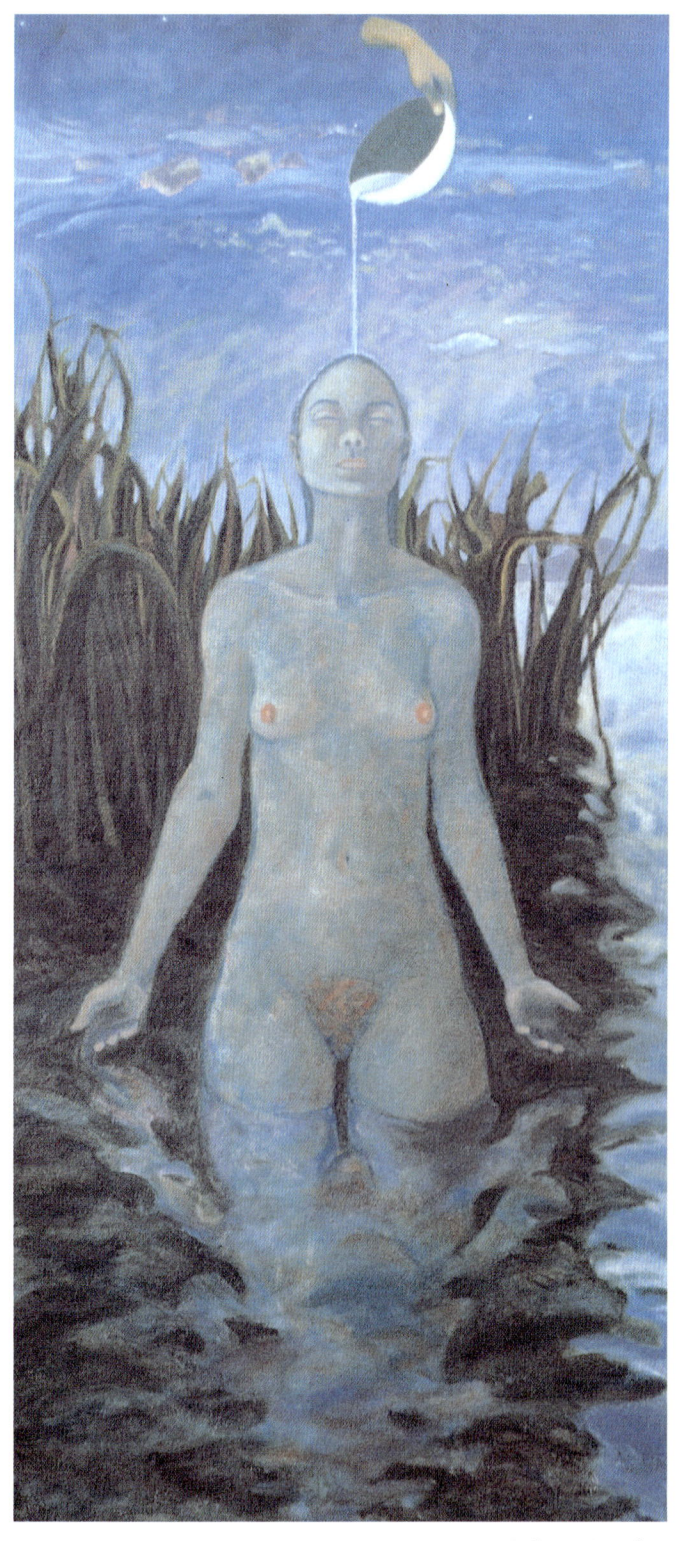

Baptism © Colette Crutcher

May

20 ☉ > ♊ 11:23a — Victoria Day (Canada)
Monday

21
Tuesday

22 ♌ 9:28a
Wednesday

23
Thursday

24 ♍ 9:58p — Shavuot
Friday

25 ◐
Saturday

26
Sunday

In the lands of the
  universe there is
  no place
Where she does not
  manifest herself ...
Compassion wondrous as
  a great cloud,
Pouring spiritual rain
  like nectar,
Quenching the flames
  of distress!
    —from *The Lotus Sutra*

May

S	M	T	W	T	F	S
			1	2	3	4
5	6	7	8	9	10	11
12	13	14	15	16	17	18
19	20	21	22	23	24	25
26	27	28	29	30	31	

June

S	M	T	W	T	F	S
						1
2	3	4	5	6	7	8
9	10	11	12	13	14	15
16	17	18	19	20	21	22
23	24	25	26	27	28	29
30						

Blodeuwedd © Jen Delyth

May & June

27 ♎ 8:33a   Memorial Day
Monday

28
Tuesday

Sing to the mystery.
Tend the garden.
—*Anne Hillman*

29 ♏ 3:30p
Wednesday

30
Thursday

31 ♐ 6:43p
Friday

1 ○
Saturday

2 ♑ 7:29p
Sunday

June

S	M	T	W	T	F	S
						1
2	3	4	5	6	7	8
9	10	11	12	13	14	15
16	17	18	19	20	21	22
23	24	25	26	27	28	29
30						

July

S	M	T	W	T	F	S
	1	2	3	4	5	6
7	8	9	10	11	12	13
14	15	16	17	18	19	20
21	22	23	24	25	26	27
28	29	30	31			

Spirit Bath © Tinker

June

3
Monday

4 ♒ 7:44p
Tuesday

5
Wednesday

6 ♓ 9:19p
Thursday

7
Friday

8 ☽
Saturday

9 ♈ 1:23a   Children's Day
Sunday

> We have the same oceans in our veins, are sisters to the trees and rocks and stars, hold their identical minerals in our bones. One family.
> —*Elsa Gidlow*

June

S	M	T	W	T	F	S
						1
2	3	4	5	6	7	8
9	10	11	12	13	14	15
16	17	18	19	20	21	22
23	24	25	26	27	28	29
30						

July

S	M	T	W	T	F	S
	1	2	3	4	5	6
7	8	9	10	11	12	13
14	15	16	17	18	19	20
21	22	23	24	25	26	27
28	29	30	31			

A Traditional Navajo Prayer

The Navajo Chantway ceremonies, among the most moving and lovely of all oral poetries, were sung mainly by men at the time of their recording by anthropologists, but were reported to have had their original source in Changing Woman, daughter of First Man and mother of the Navajo people. The selection below is from the female branch of the Shootingway ceremony, used to cure illnesses caused by lightning, snakes, or arrows. The nine-day-and-night-long sing from which it comes was performed by a medicine man named Red-Point for the benefit of his daughter Marie. This prayer was repeated four times in front of a carefully selected young pinon tree as the final act of the ceremony.

—Jane Hirschfield

Dark young pine, at the center of the earth originating,
    I have made your sacrifice.
Whiteshell, turquoise, abalone beautiful,
Jet beautiful, fool's gold beautiful, blue pollen beautiful,
    reed pollen, pollen beautiful, your sacrifice I have made.
This day your child I have become, I say.

Watch over me.
Hold your hand before me in protection.
Stand guard for me, speak in defense of me.
As I speak for you, speak for me.
As you speak for me, so will I speak for you.
    May it be beautiful before me,
    May it be beautiful behind me,
    May it be beautiful below me,
    May it be beautiful above me,
    May it be beautiful all around me.

    I am restored in beauty.
    I am restored in beauty.
    I am restored in beauty.
    I am restored in beauty.

(translated by Gladys A. Reichard)

June

10
Monday

11 ♂ 8:11a
Tuesday

12
Wednesday

13 ♊ 5:16p
Thursday

14
Friday

15 ●
Saturday

16 ♋ 4:08a   Father's Day
Sunday

June

S	M	T	W	T	F	S
						1
2	3	4	5	6	7	8
9	10	11	12	13	14	15
16	17	18	19	20	21	22
23	24	25	26	27	28	29
30						

July

S	M	T	W	T	F	S
	1	2	3	4	5	6
7	8	9	10	11	12	13
14	15	16	17	18	19	20
21	22	23	24	25	26	27
28	29	30	31			

Woman With Shaman's Drum © Melissa Harris

June

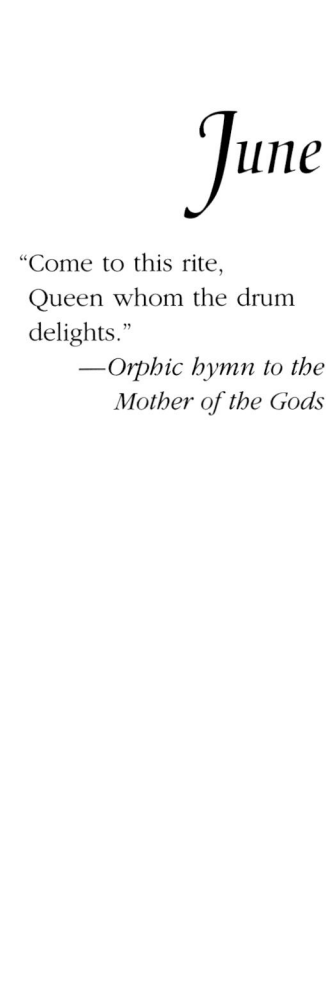

17
Monday

"Come to this rite,
Queen whom the drum
delights."
—*Orphic hymn to the
Mother of the Gods*

18 ♌ 4:22p
Tuesday

19
Wednesday

Juneteenth—African American Emancipation

20 ☉ > ♋ 7:24p
Thursday

Summer Solstice

21 ♍ 5:06a
Friday

22
Saturday

23 ♎ 4:37p ◑
Sunday

June

S	M	T	W	T	F	S
						1
2	3	4	5	6	7	8
9	10	11	12	13	14	15
16	17	18	19	20	21	22
23	24	25	26	27	28	29
30						

July

S	M	T	W	T	F	S
	1	2	3	4	5	6
7	8	9	10	11	12	13
14	15	16	17	18	19	20
21	22	23	24	25	26	27
28	29	30	31			

Summertime Valerian Wine

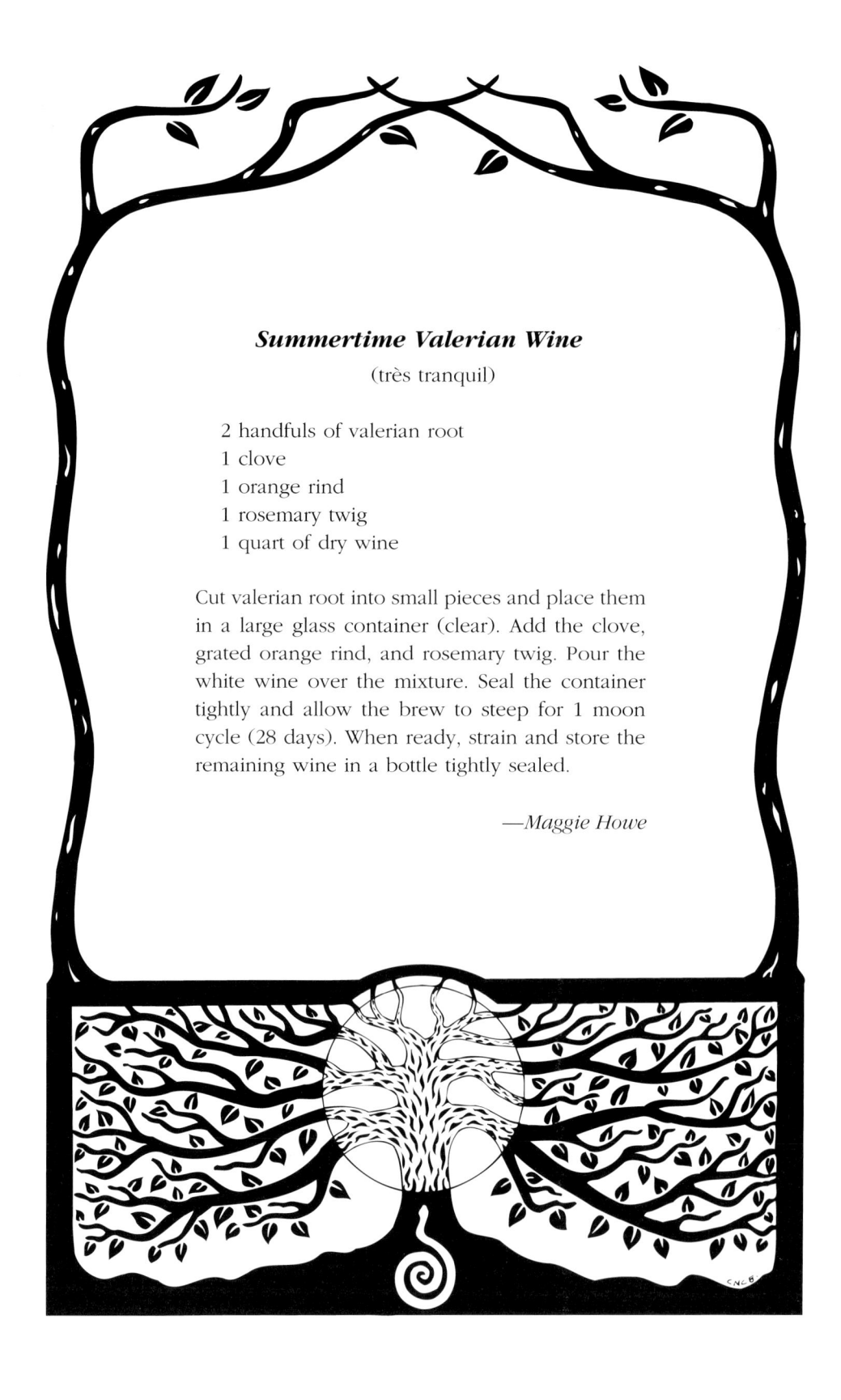

(très tranquil)

2 handfuls of valerian root
1 clove
1 orange rind
1 rosemary twig
1 quart of dry wine

Cut valerian root into small pieces and place them in a large glass container (clear). Add the clove, grated orange rind, and rosemary twig. Pour the white wine over the mixture. Seal the container tightly and allow the brew to steep for 1 moon cycle (28 days). When ready, strain and store the remaining wine in a bottle tightly sealed.

—*Maggie Howe*

June

24
Monday

25
Tuesday

26 ♏ 12:53a
Wednesday

27
Thursday

28 ♐ 5:01a
Friday

29
Saturday

30 ♑ 5:47a ○
Sunday

June

S	M	T	W	T	F	S
						1
2	3	4	5	6	7	8
9	10	11	12	13	14	15
16	17	18	19	20	21	22
23	24	25	26	27	28	29
30						

July

S	M	T	W	T	F	S
	1	2	3	4	5	6
7	8	9	10	11	12	13
14	15	16	17	18	19	20
21	22	23	24	25	26	27
28	29	30	31			

Shaman © Jaye Oliver

*J*uly

1
Monday — Canada Day

2 ♒ 5:05a
Tuesday

3
Wednesday

4 ♓ 5:07a — Independence Day
Thursday

5
Friday

6 ♈ 7:42a
Saturday

7 ◐
Sunday

Ask within for her
 advice,
She is the Mother
 of the Ages,
Nothing surprises her.
She has seen it all.
 —*Clarissa Pinkola Estés*

July

S	M	T	W	T	F	S
	1	2	3	4	5	6
7	8	9	10	11	12	13
14	15	16	17	18	19	20
21	22	23	24	25	26	27
28	29	30	31			

August

S	M	T	W	T	F	S
				1	2	3
4	5	6	7	8	9	10
11	12	13	14	15	16	17
18	19	20	21	22	23	24
25	26	27	28	29	30	31

*W*e are earth stuff, a geological formation. Handfuls of magma and mud given form over time. Built on the vertebrae of fishes, fired by the rituals of serpents, standing on the shoulders of mice. Deep with the dimension of thought, we are loved by life, nurtured with all that is needed.

—Anne Hillman

July

8 ♉ 1:43p
Monday

9
Tuesday

10 ♊ 10:52p
Wednesday

11
Thursday

12
Friday

13 ♋ 10:08a Our Lady of Fatima (Portugal)
Saturday

14
Sunday

July

S	M	T	W	T	F	S
	1	2	3	4	5	6
7	8	9	10	11	12	13
14	15	16	17	18	19	20
21	22	23	24	25	26	27
28	29	30	31			

August

S	M	T	W	T	F	S
				1	2	3
4	5	6	7	8	9	10
11	12	13	14	15	16	17
18	19	20	21	22	23	24
25	26	27	28	29	30	31

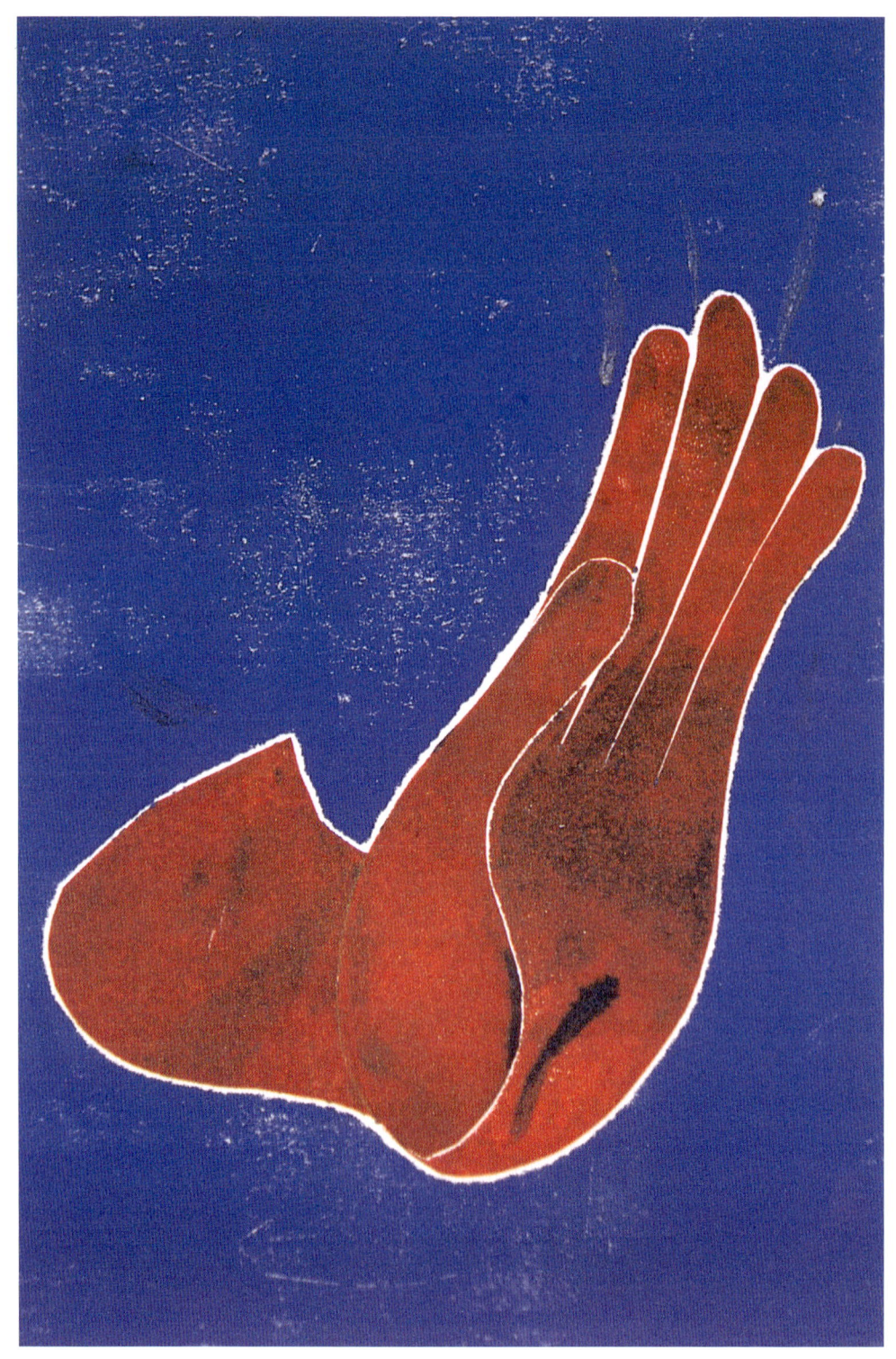

Dispelling Fear © Nina Mullen

July

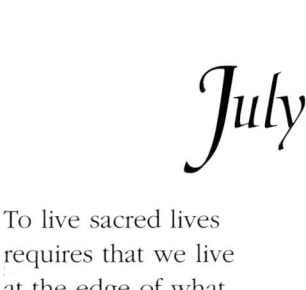

15 ♌ 10:31p ●
Monday

To live sacred lives
requires that we live
at the edge of what
we do not know.
—*Anne Hillman*

16
Tuesday

17   Feast of Amaterasu (Japan)
Wednesday

18 ♍ 11:16a
Thursday

19
Friday

20 ♎ 11:14p
Saturday

21
Sunday

July

S	M	T	W	T	F	S
		1	2	3	4	5	6
7	8	9	10	11	12	13
14	15	16	17	18	19	20
21	22	23	24	25	26	27
28	29	30	31			

August

S	M	T	W	T	F	S
				1	2	3
4	5	6	7	8	9	10
11	12	13	14	15	16	17
18	19	20	21	22	23	24
25	26	27	28	29	30	31

Make for yourself a medicine bag. It may be a bag that has been in your family, possibly your mother's or grandmother's. I chose for my medicine bag a woven southwestern Native American bag that my mother gave to me when I was 18. For my daughter's rite of passage ceremony at the age of 13, my mother made her a white doeskin bag that she beaded with beautiful red and blue glass trade beads. You may want to make your own bag from fabrics that have special meaning to you—perhaps a favorite piece of clothing from childhood.

Put in your bag photos of your loved ones. Begin with your ancestors. I have a photo of my grandparents on my father's side picnicking in a southern California canyon in the 1920s. When I look at it, I feel the strength and earthiness I have inherited from these wild pioneers who drove from their home in Michigan in 5 cars to California in 1923, camping along the way. (With flat tires every day, three cars made it. Two were left behind.)

Choose photos of yourself at different ages—find pictures where you are extremely happy, joyful, ecstatic, in your power. If you don't have any, create a ceremony for yourself, invite your closest friends and ask them to photograph you.

Place these photographs in your medicine bag. In those inevitable moments when you are confused, lost or frightened, these photos will encourage and center you. They will remind you of your deeper self and help you reconnect to essence. They are powerful medicine.

Put prayers into the bag. You will know what else to put in there.

Your medicine bag will help you to remember the woman you truly are and the extraordinary woman you are becoming.

—*Claudia L'Amoreaux*

July

22 ☉ > ♌ 6:19a
Monday

23 ♏ 8:43a ◐
Tuesday

24
Wednesday

25 ♐ 2:24p
Thursday

26
Friday

27 ♑ 4:17p
Saturday

28
Sunday

						July
S	M	T	W	T	F	S
	1	2	3	4	5	6
7	8	9	10	11	12	13
14	15	16	17	18	19	20
21	22	23	24	25	26	27
28	29	30	31			

						August
S	M	T	W	T	F	S
				1	2	3
4	5	6	7	8	9	10
11	12	13	14	15	16	17
18	19	20	21	22	23	24
25	26	27	28	29	30	31

Birth, Peace Over Gaia © Diana Vandenberg

July & August

29 ♒ 3:47p
Monday

30 ○
Tuesday

31 ♓ 3:00p
Wednesday

1
Thursday

2 ♈ 4:05p   Lammas
Friday

3
Saturday

4 ♉ 8:33p
Sunday

> I believe in the
>   Holy Spirit*
> as she moves over
>   the waters
> of creation
> and over the earth
> —Rachel Walberg
>
> *The Hebrew word for
> Spirit is feminine.

August

S	M	T	W	T	F	S
				1	2	3
4	5	6	7	8	9	10
11	12	13	14	15	16	17
18	19	20	21	22	23	24
25	26	27	28	29	30	31

September

S	M	T	W	T	F	S
1	2	3	4	5	6	7
8	9	10	11	12	13	14
15	16	17	18	19	20	21
22	23	24	25	26	27	28
29	30					

The Great Tree

I am the Great Tree.
My roots go deep to delve the dark places.
The sound of the waters,
the compact wisdom
of the rocks,
I know their secrets.
I am committed, steadfast.
I experience joy where I stand.
I know the inexpressible glory of the moment.
I worship in faultless bliss
and I am singing.
My hair is filled with sunlight and
I feel the winds of change—
they flow through me,
I am moved but
I stay where I am.
I know my place is perfect—
this moment, this moment is
perfect.
And I am singing.
I stretch my arms to receive them,
the lives, all who come,
I offer them shelter.
They nourish me with their sweet droppings,
their leavings,
they come and go
and I stay
singing the story,
weaving the threads of
Earth and Sky, Earth and Sky, Earth and Sky and
Sky and Earth.
And I am singing.

—*Ellen Evert Hopman*

August

5 ◐
Monday

6
Tuesday

7 ♊ 4:49a
Wednesday

8 Tij Day—Women's Day (Nepal)
Thursday

9 ♋ 3:57p
Friday

10
Saturday

11
Sunday

August

S	M	T	W	T	F	S
				1	2	3
4	5	6	7	8	9	10
11	12	13	14	15	16	17
18	19	20	21	22	23	24
25	26	27	28	29	30	31

September

S	M	T	W	T	F	S
1	2	3	4	5	6	7
8	9	10	11	12	13	14
15	16	17	18	19	20	21
22	23	24	25	26	27	28
29	30					

Mamala, the Surf Rider © Mayumi Oda

August

12 ♌ 4:29a
Monday

13
Tuesday

14 ♍ 5:07p ●
Wednesday

15 Birthday of Isis (North Africa)
Thursday

16
Friday

17 ♎ 4:55a
Saturday

18
Sunday

> Tell me what is it you plan to do with your one wild and precious life?
> —*Mary Oliver*

August

S	M	T	W	T	F	S
					1	2	3
4	5	6	7	8	9	10
11	12	13	14	15	16	17
18	19	20	21	22	23	24
25	26	27	28	29	30	31

September

S	M	T	W	T	F	S
	1	2	3	4	5	6	7
8	9	10	11	12	13	14
15	16	17	18	19	20	21
22	23	24	25	26	27	28
29	30					

Wise Woman Way

These are the ways of our ancient grandmothers, the ancient ones who still live. These wise women spin the invisible web which weaves us all together. They invite you to weave the threads of your own life back into the cloak of the ancient one, the holy blanket of the wise woman. They thank you for reweaving, wherever you can, the sacred threads of planetary, animal, plant, and personal kinship.

These are the ways of our ancient grandmothers, the ancient ones who still live. The joy of life is the give-away. They give you a gift of a robe, a robe woven of unconditional self-love: luminous, resonant, shimmering.

Here, put it on. Ah! Do you feel it?

As you emerge through the neckhole you become the center of the universe. All revolves around you, the world's axis, life's matrix, the still point in the ever-moving. The designs of the universe itself radiate down your sleeves and bodice. It is an ancient design. Lift your arms. You are the tree of life, the goddess, unique and whole.

And as you trace the invisible way of the Wise Woman, wearing your robe, know that the ancient ones offer you safe journey. They offer you safe journey and the possibility of finding yourself healthy/whole/holy. This is the Wise Woman way the world round.

—*Susun Weed*

August

19 ♏ 2:50p
Monday

20
Tuesday

21 ♐ 9:48p ☾
Wednesday

22 ☉ > ♍ 1:23p
Thursday

23
Friday

24 ♑ 1:22a
Saturday

25
Sunday

August

S	M	T	W	T	F	S
				1	2	3
4	5	6	7	8	9	10
11	12	13	14	15	16	17
18	19	20	21	22	23	24
25	26	27	28	29	30	31

September

S	M	T	W	T	F	S
1	2	3	4	5	6	7
8	9	10	11	12	13	14
15	16	17	18	19	20	21
22	23	24	25	26	27	28
29	30					

On Wall Building

Walls are our opponents and our strength.

There is the *Kotel*, the Western Wall in Jerusalem, where women are forbidden to pray in a group, to sing loudly, to have the Torah.

But I believe we must build walls everywhere like giant bulletin boards: our own prayer walls, beseeching walls, requesting walls ...

And we would sing at our walls:

Mound of mothers,
height of the past,
offerings piled like autumn leaves,
masonry of memory,
cementing our lives,
oh, retainer, hold us, hear us,
let our whispers roar,
let the walls of silence be broken
as women wish together.

—*E.M. Broner*
excerpt from Ceremonies to Go

August & September

26 ♒ 2:10a
Monday

27
Tuesday

28 ♓ 1:49a ○
Wednesday

29
Thursday

30 ♈ 2:15a
Friday

31
Saturday

1 ♉ 5:19a   Radha's Day (Indian)
Sunday

September

S	M	T	W	T	F	S
1	2	3	4	5	6	7
8	9	10	11	12	13	14
15	16	17	18	19	20	21
22	23	24	25	26	27	28
29	30					

October

S	M	T	W	T	F	S
		1	2	3	4	5
6	7	8	9	10	11	12
13	14	15	16	17	18	19
20	21	22	23	24	25	26
27	28	29	30	31		

Grace

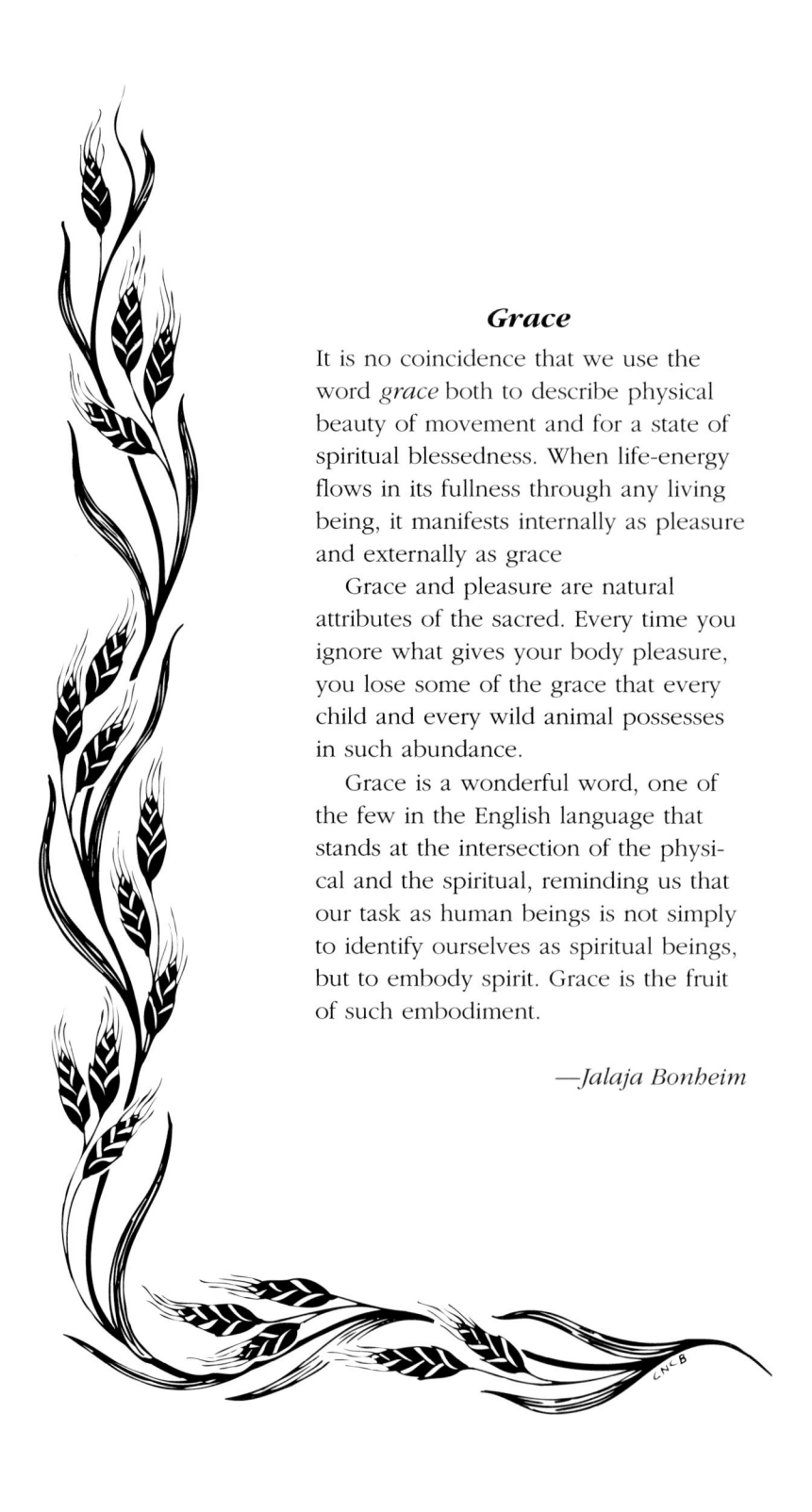

It is no coincidence that we use the word *grace* both to describe physical beauty of movement and for a state of spiritual blessedness. When life-energy flows in its fullness through any living being, it manifests internally as pleasure and externally as grace

Grace and pleasure are natural attributes of the sacred. Every time you ignore what gives your body pleasure, you lose some of the grace that every child and every wild animal possesses in such abundance.

Grace is a wonderful word, one of the few in the English language that stands at the intersection of the physical and the spiritual, reminding us that our task as human beings is not simply to identify ourselves as spiritual beings, but to embody spirit. Grace is the fruit of such embodiment.

—*Jalaja Bonheim*

September

2 — Labor Day
Monday

3 ♊ 12:08p
Tuesday

4 ☽
Wednesday

5 ♋ 10:29p
Thursday

6
Friday

7
Saturday

8 ♌ 10:54a
Sunday

September

S	M	T	W	T	F	S
	1	2	3	4	5	6	7
8	9	10	11	12	13	14
15	16	17	18	19	20	21
22	23	24	25	26	27	28
29	30					

October

S	M	T	W	T	F	S
		1	2	3	4	5
6	7	8	9	10	11	12
13	14	15	16	17	18	19
20	21	22	23	24	25	26
27	28	29	30	31		

Center Oak © Hue Walker

September

9
Monday

10 ♍ 11:28p
Tuesday

11
Wednesday

12 ●
Thursday

13 ♎ 10:51a
Friday

14 Rosh Hashanah begins at sundown (Jewish New Year)
Saturday

15 ♏ 8:20p
Sunday

Slip into the bark-skin,
reach into the soil
  and, with wandering,
  myriad rootlets,
search the nether places.
—*Hue Walker*

September

S	M	T	W	T	F	S
1	2	3	4	5	6	7
8	9	10	11	12	13	14
15	16	17	18	19	20	21
22	23	24	25	26	27	28
29	30					

October

S	M	T	W	T	F	S
		1	2	3	4	5
6	7	8	9	10	11	12
13	14	15	16	17	18	19
20	21	22	23	24	25	26
27	28	29	30	31		

Medicine Woman © Ruth Zachary

September

16 Monday — Independence Day (Mexico)

17 Tuesday

18 ♐ 3:31a
Wednesday

19 Thursday

20 ♑ 8:12a ☽
Friday

21 Saturday — Rites of Eleusis (Greece)

22 ♒ 10:39a ☉ > ♎ 11:00a — Autumn Equinox
Sunday

Woman of a sacred, enchanted place am I ...
Mujer del lugar sagrado y encantado soy ...
—María Sabina, Sacred Mushroom Shaman (July 22, 1884- October 31, 1987)

September

S	M	T	W	T	F	S
1	2	3	4	5	6	7
8	9	10	11	12	13	14
15	16	17	18	19	20	21
22	23	24	25	26	27	28
29	30					

October

S	M	T	W	T	F	S
		1	2	3	4	5
6	7	8	9	10	11	12
13	14	15	16	17	18	19
20	21	22	23	24	25	26
27	28	29	30	31		

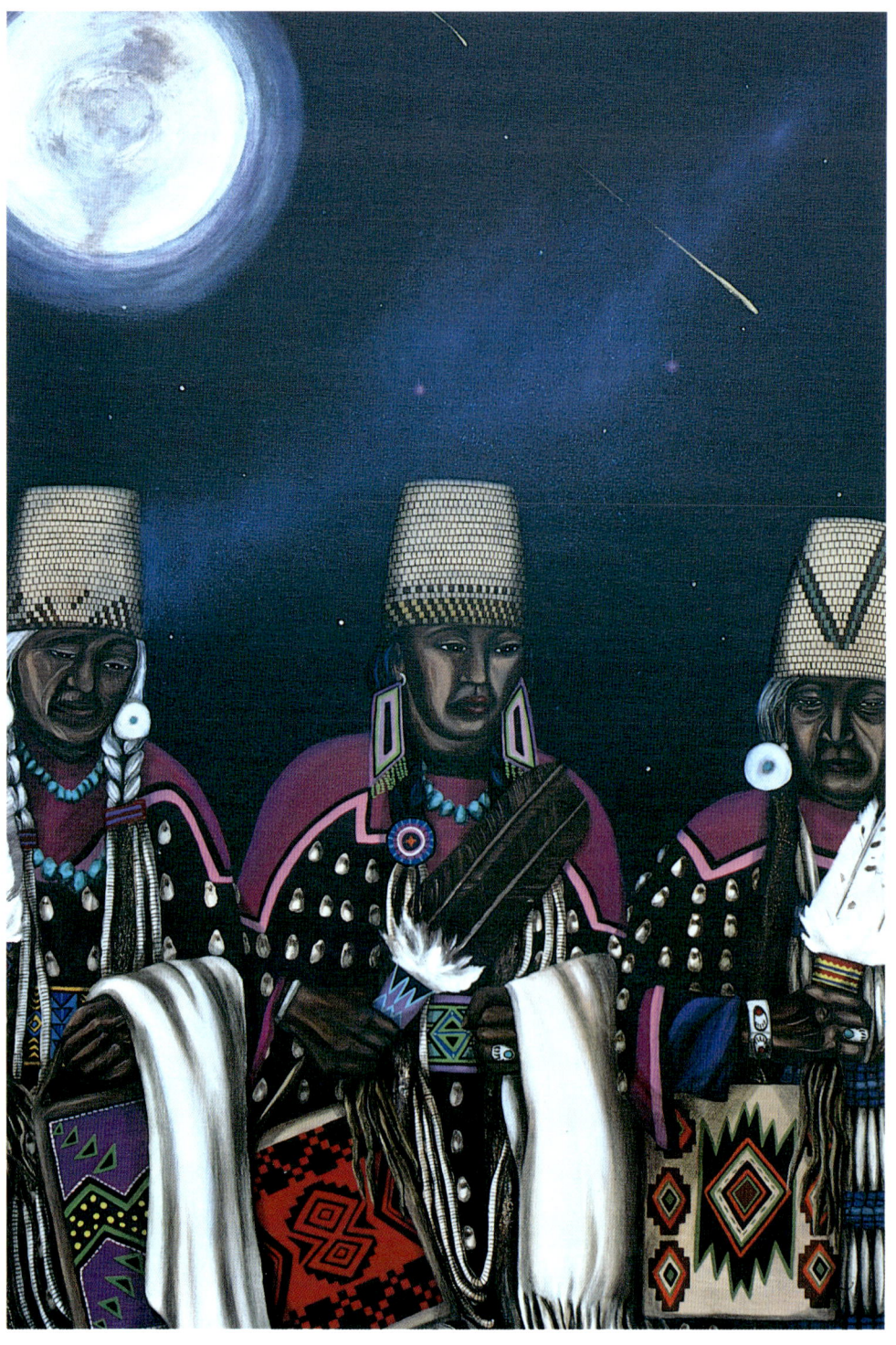

Wasco Clan Bearers © Susana Santos

September

23
Monday — Yom Kippur (Day of Atonement, Jewish)

24 ♓ 11:43a
Tuesday

25
Wednesday

26 ♈ 12:45p ○
Thursday

27
Friday

28 ♉ 3:23p
Saturday

29
Sunday

Let us join hands and pray, as we may never have prayed before:

"Our Mother, who is in heaven ..."
—*Louis Cunha*

September

S	M	T	W	T	F	S
1	2	3	4	5	6	7
8	9	10	11	12	13	14
15	16	17	18	19	20	21
22	23	24	25	26	27	28
29	30					

October

S	M	T	W	T	F	S
		1	2	3	4	5
6	7	8	9	10	11	12
13	14	15	16	17	18	19
20	21	22	23	24	25	26
27	28	29	30	31		

Spell to Send Away Mal Occhio

Tomato sauce bubbles
in the big, black pot
Grandma stirs
with her long, wooden
spoon.
The scent of garlic
circles the room—
protection in the kitchen.
Pasta waits.
Grandma sits me
at the table,
draws the shades,
the room is gray.
Grandma lights the candles,
places a small bowl
of olive oil and water
on the table,
rubs the oil
on my forehead and
prays to the Madonna.
My headache is gone.
Now we eat.

—Rose Romano
(Mal occhio: evil eye)

September
&
October

30 ♊ 9:01p
Monday

1
Tuesday

2
Wednesday

3 ♋ 6:14a
Thursday

4 ◐
Friday

5 ♌ 6:12p   Sophia's Day (Greece)
Saturday

6
Sunday

October

S	M	T	W	T	F	S
			1	2	3	4	5
6	7	8	9	10	11	12
13	14	15	16	17	18	19
20	21	22	23	24	25	26
27	28	29	30	31		

November

S	M	T	W	T	F	S
					1	2
3	4	5	6	7	8	9
10	11	12	13	14	15	16
17	18	19	20	21	22	23
24	25	26	27	28	29	30

Dunham's Life Song © Asungi

October

7
Monday

8 ♍ 6:48a
Tuesday

9
Wednesday

10 ♎ 6:00p
Thursday

11
Friday

12 ●
Saturday

13 ♏ 2:45a
Sunday

Watching the moon
at midnight,
solitary, mid-sky,
I knew myself
   completely,
no part left out.
—*Izumi Shikibu*
(974-1034)

October

S	M	T	W	T	F	S
		1	2	3	4	5
6	7	8	9	10	11	12
13	14	15	16	17	18	19
20	21	22	23	24	25	26
27	28	29	30	31		

November

S	M	T	W	T	F	S
					1	2
3	4	5	6	7	8	9
10	11	12	13	14	15	16
17	18	19	20	21	22	23
24	25	26	27	28	29	30

The white bark is peeled from the birch. The layers pulled apart. A piece is folded in half and then half again. nvuelzjch takes the point of it in her mouth. She bites along the fold. Eyeteeth against side-teeth. She chews a geometric design in the papery bark. A braille of sorts. Something like a large snowflake when she unfolds it. Maybe the pattern of woodland blizzards still in her head. The old woman has chewed so long her teeth are gone. The spirits come to her in bifocals. Together they enter the chaos before creation. They feel their way back through the dark. The birch-bark biter hears the ancestors in their graves. Sometimes they grind their teeth in sleep. She holds to the spirit ahead of her. Her dentures now chewing. Does it matter the earth has changed? nvuelzjch still has the journey, bringing her bitings from the dark.

—Diane Glancy

October

14   Thanksgiving (Canada)
Monday

15 ♐ 9:07a
Tuesday

16
Wednesday

17 ♑ 1:37p
Thursday

18
Friday

19 ♒ 4:51p ☽
Saturday

20
Sunday

October

S	M	T	W	T	F	S
		1	2	3	4	5
6	7	8	9	10	11	12
13	14	15	16	17	18	19
20	21	22	23	24	25	26
27	28	29	30	31		

November

S	M	T	W	T	F	S
					1	2
3	4	5	6	7	8	9
10	11	12	13	14	15	16
17	18	19	20	21	22	23
24	25	26	27	28	29	30

Remedios © Amy Córdova

October

21 ♓ 7:22p
Monday

22 ☉ > ♏ 8:19p
Tuesday

23 ♈ 9:50p
Wednesday

24
Thursday

25
Friday

26 ♉ 1:11a ○
Saturday

27
Sunday

GRANDMOTHER, where do I begin? What thread begins the yarn? What story begins the weave?

Begin with the stirring, begin with the stirring in your own dark center, begin ...
—*Gwendolyn Endicott*

October

S	M	T	W	T	F	S
		1	2	3	4	5
6	7	8	9	10	11	12
13	14	15	16	17	18	19
20	21	22	23	24	25	26
27	28	29	30	31		

November

S	M	T	W	T	F	S
					1	2
3	4	5	6	7	8	9
10	11	12	13	14	15	16
17	18	19	20	21	22	23
24	25	26	27	28	29	30

𝓘magine the Gossips, the Gorgons, and Crones standing over a raging fire in the dead of night. Hanging above that dragon fire is a giant cauldron that changes colors from purple to silver to copper to red and finally to black. The Gossips are muttering among themselves. The Gorgons are gazing deeply into the black hole of the cauldron's eye. The Crones are waving large crooked sticks over its surface, stirring up trouble, brewing up brainstorms, reconstituting creation.

The cauldron is the magical matrix of Chaos into which all the structures by which we have been ruled and controlled for millennia are now crackling, cracking, and dissolving. Peer with your owl eyes into the rising, infinitely turbulent steam. Actively visualize what is now bubbling forth. Become fateful, taking responsibility for what turn our world is now taking.

—Jane Caputi

October & November

28 ♊ 5:34a
Monday

29
Tuesday

30 ♋ 1:56p — Daylight Saving Time ends
Wednesday

31 — Halloween
Thursday

1 — Feast of the Dead (Mexico)
Friday

2 ♌ 1:16a ◐
Saturday

3
Sunday

November

S	M	T	W	T	F	S
					1	2
3	4	5	6	7	8	9
10	11	12	13	14	15	16
17	18	19	20	21	22	23
24	25	26	27	28	29	30

December

S	M	T	W	T	F	S
	1	2	3	4	5	6	7
8	9	10	11	12	13	14
15	16	17	18	19	20	21
22	23	24	25	26	27	28
29	30	31				

Healer Crone © Megaera

November

4 ♍ 1:57p
Monday

5
Tuesday General Election Day

6
Wednesday

7 ♎ 1:29a
Thursday

8
Friday

9 ♏ 10:02a
Saturday

10 ●
Sunday

Come old one
Mountain crone
Give us your wisdom
Come moon
Give us your kiss
of silver ...
—*Shekhinah Mountainwater*

November

S	M	T	W	T	F	S
					1	2
3	4	5	6	7	8	9
10	11	12	13	14	15	16
17	18	19	20	21	22	23
24	25	26	27	28	29	30

December

S	M	T	W	T	F	S
1	2	3	4	5	6	7
8	9	10	11	12	13	14
15	16	17	18	19	20	21
22	23	24	25	26	27	28
29	30	31				

Wild Crones Meet

I wake before to a room full—
big-breasted and little, many European,
many black-skinned, all speaking
with accents. I find the head one,
reach out three times to touch her arm,
high up, heart-side. Fourth time
she bats my hand away,
sits herself down in an easy-chair
and bares her chest,
fingers fanning out over the breast-fold
near the shoulder. She's showing us
how to hold our hearts, to open them wider.
Some old ones start chanting, and the chant
catches on, all different chants mingling,
yet I'm still not singing.
I tell the heart-teacher,
softly, in her ear,
Have each one who knows
teach her song to one just beginning.

—Rosie King-Smyth

November

11 ♐ 3:26p   Remembrance Day (Canada)
Monday

12
Tuesday

13 ♑ 6:44p
Wednesday

14
Thursday

15 ♒ 9:14p
Friday

16
Saturday

17 ♓ 10:00p ☽
Sunday

November

S	M	T	W	T	F	S
					1	2
3	4	5	6	7	8	9
10	11	12	13	14	15	16
17	18	19	20	21	22	23
24	25	26	27	28	29	30

December

S	M	T	W	T	F	S
1	2	3	4	5	6	7
8	9	10	11	12	13	14
15	16	17	18	19	20	21
22	23	24	25	26	27	28
29	30	31				

Gathering strength for the inner journey
© Cynthia Cunningham-Baxter

November

18
Monday

19
Tuesday

20 ♈ 3:34a
Wednesday

21 ☉ > ♐ 4:50p
Thursday

22 ♉ 8:12a
Friday

23
Saturday

24 ♊ 2:20p ○
Sunday

Frog
Guardian of Chac*
jumped so high
she reached the moon
and brought a piece back.
Ever since, the moon
has reflected
over the waters.
—*Marta Ayala*
**Chac is the Mayan*
god of water

November

S	M	T	W	T	F	S
					1	2
3	4	5	6	7	8	9
10	11	12	13	14	15	16
17	18	19	20	21	22	23
24	25	26	27	28	29	30

December

S	M	T	W	T	F	S
1	2	3	4	5	6	7
8	9	10	11	12	13	14
15	16	17	18	19	20	21
22	23	24	25	26	27	28
29	30	31				

A Feminist version of the DOXOLOGY

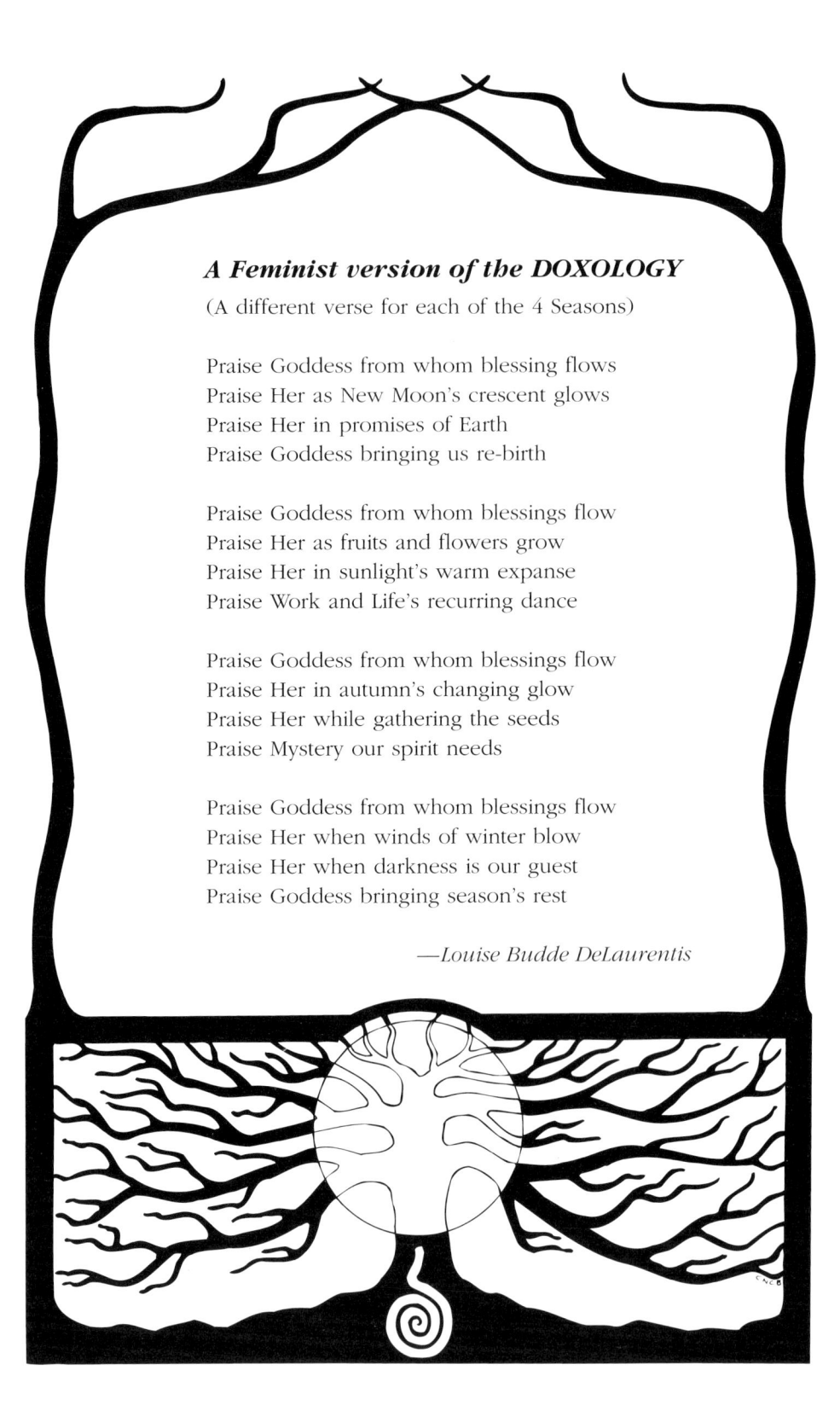

(A different verse for each of the 4 Seasons)

Praise Goddess from whom blessing flows
Praise Her as New Moon's crescent glows
Praise Her in promises of Earth
Praise Goddess bringing us re-birth

Praise Goddess from whom blessings flow
Praise Her as fruits and flowers grow
Praise Her in sunlight's warm expanse
Praise Work and Life's recurring dance

Praise Goddess from whom blessings flow
Praise Her in autumn's changing glow
Praise Her while gathering the seeds
Praise Mystery our spirit needs

Praise Goddess from whom blessings flow
Praise Her when winds of winter blow
Praise Her when darkness is our guest
Praise Goddess bringing season's rest

—*Louise Budde DeLaurentis*

November & December

25
Monday

26 ⊙ 10:37p
Tuesday

27
Wednesday

28 Thanksgiving Day
Thursday

29 ♌ 9:30a
Friday

30
Saturday

1 ♍ 10:11p
Sunday

December

S	M	T	W	T	F	S
	1	2	3	4	5	6	7
8	9	10	11	12	13	14
15	16	17	18	19	20	21
22	23	24	25	26	27	28
29	30	31				

January

S	M	T	W	T	F	S
			1	2	3	4
5	6	7	8	9	10	11
12	13	14	15	16	17	18
19	20	21	22	23	24	25
26	27	28	29	30	31	

Wolf Totem © Ruth Zachary

December

2 ☽
Monday

3
Tuesday

4 ♎ 10:23a
Wednesday

5
Thursday

6 ♏ 7:38p 1st Day of Chanukah (Festival of Lights, Jewish)
Friday

7
Saturday

8
Sunday

Faith took her deep into the woods,
   Sat her down,
and asked her to follow her heart.
—*Melissa Harris*

December

S	M	T	W	T	F	S
1	2	3	4	5	6	7
8	9	10	11	12	13	14
15	16	17	18	19	20	21
22	23	24	25	26	27	28
29	30	31				

January

S	M	T	W	T	F	S
			1	2	3	4
5	6	7	8	9	10	11
12	13	14	15	16	17	18
19	20	21	22	23	24	25
26	27	28	29	30	31	

Arianrhod © Jen Delyth

December

9 ♐ 12:58a
Monday

10 ●
Tuesday

11 ♑ 3:14a
Wednesday

12
Thursday

13 ♒ 4:14a   St. Lucia Day (Sweden)
Friday

14
Saturday

15 ♓ 5:44a
Sunday

Wisdom of stars
and galaxies
and universes
grant me vision.
—*Louise Budde
DeLaurentis*

December

S	M	T	W	T	F	S
1	2	3	4	5	6	7
8	9	10	11	12	13	14
15	16	17	18	19	20	21
22	23	24	25	26	27	28
29	30	31				

January

S	M	T	W	T	F	S
			1	2	3	4
5	6	7	8	9	10	11
12	13	14	15	16	17	18
19	20	21	22	23	24	25
26	27	28	29	30	31	

I was alone. Yet, as I added twigs and dry boughs, then madrone logs, the firelit room became peopled by presences: spirits of women. Women I had known: mother, grandmother, elder aunts, and back, back, back, all the women through the ages who had kindled and tended sacred and domestic fires. The elements that feel to me most kindred are water and earth. Fire seemed an opposite power, yet fascinating. That dusk of my fortieth year I began to see why.

My thought revolved around the recent transitions of my life: from city to country, concrete to earth, from rented flat to my own space, from the death of a beloved and a tumultuous relationship to solitude. As the rain poured down and the storm shook the small redwood house, there was born the possibility of a joyous sense of *connectedness*. A tilting storm-battered house, an emotionally and economically precarious era, at the doorstep of midlife with no obvious achievement other than survival: none of them mattered. Deeply inward, something new was happening.

I watched the burning madrone logs contribute to one another's glow, each keeping the other alight. I again felt the presence of the women who had been familiars of this element. I heard their voices telling me: "This fire on your hearth is neither individual nor separate any more than your living self is separate from us. We are part of one another as your small blaze is part of our chains of fires linking the centuries, a spark of the cosmic element itself."

For a moment, I wondered … fire not a separate element? Then I saw. This fire I had lighted included earth, air, water, and my human agency. The wood that nourished it included the tree's nurturing earth, the water that had made its food available, the air without which it could not live or burn. The flame on my hearth was composite of all the elements. I comprehended why it was a symbol of the sacred. Before going to bed, I placed more logs on the glowing coals of the evening fire.

In the morning, the first dawn of my renewed life, the still smoldering cores of the logs seemed telling me what to do. Madrone wood burns like coal. I placed it on a metal dustpan and took the logs out into the gently rainy morning, there to become charcoal as they quickly ceased consuming themselves. When the remains of my Solstice Fire had cooled, I wrapped them in foil, tied with a piece of red ribbon and placed them on a shelf above the growing woodpile. This became the first of all the subsequent Solstice Fire Logs, each to kindle the next, for all the years of my life, up to the present.

—*Elsa Gidlow*

December

16
Monday

17 ♈ 8:55a ☽
Tuesday

18
Wednesday

19 ♉ 2:09p
Thursday

20
Friday

21 ♊ 9:17p ☉ > ♑ 6:06p   Winter Solstice
Saturday

22
Sunday

December

S	M	T	W	T	F	S
	1	2	3	4	5	6	7
8	9	10	11	12	13	14
15	16	17	18	19	20	21
22	23	24	25	26	27	28
29	30	31				

January

S	M	T	W	T	F	S
			1	2	3	4
5	6	7	8	9	10	11
12	13	14	15	16	17	18
19	20	21	22	23	24	25
26	27	28	29	30	31	

$\mathcal{I}$f you were to live to be ninety years old, what year would it be? I will be ninety in 2044. My mother will be ninety in 2015. My daughter will be ninety in 2069.

Close your eyes. Take yourself into the future, to the year of your ninetieth birthday, whatever year that may be. Now imagine a space that you might go to for ceremony, counsel, healing. See it in your mind's eye, vividly. Where is it located? What shape is it? What materials is it made of? What source of energy powers it? How does the water taste? Where does it come from? Are there trees there? What kinds? How old are these trees?

Now imagine a ninety-year-old crone is the caretaker of this healing space—she is you in the future—your wisest, loving crone-self. See her in front of you now, walking towards you. Look into her eyes. Feel the love she has for you, the tenderness and compassion.

Tell her what is on your mind. Tell her what is in your heart. Let her share with you her counsel. Let her touch you with her healer's hands. Let her sing you the songs that have come to her as gifts from the spirit world. When you open your eyes, bring back a song.

—*Claudia L'Amoreaux*

December

23
Monday

24 ♋ 6:14a ○
Tuesday

25 Christmas
Wednesday

26 ♌ 5:09p First Day of Kwanzaa (African American)
Thursday

27
Friday

28
Saturday

29 ♍ 5:45a
Sunday

December

S	M	T	W	T	F	S
1	2	3	4	5	6	7
8	9	10	11	12	13	14
15	16	17	18	19	20	21
22	23	24	25	26	27	28
29	30	31				

January

S	M	T	W	T	F	S
			1	2	3	4
5	6	7	8	9	10	11
12	13	14	15	16	17	18
19	20	21	22	23	24	25
26	27	28	29	30	31	

Mother and Child © Lee Lawson

December & January

30
Monday

31 ♎ 6:32p
Tuesday

1 New Year's Day '97
Wednesday

2 ◐
Thursday

3 ♏ 5:02a
Friday

4
Saturday

5 ♐ 11:27a
Sunday

"Blessed be
all that you think
all that you feel
all that you do."
—*Karen Ethelsdattar
& Ann Doemland*

December

S	M	T	W	T	F	S
1	2	3	4	5	6	7
8	9	10	11	12	13	14
15	16	17	18	19	20	21
22	23	24	25	26	27	28
29	30	31				

January

S	M	T	W	T	F	S
			1	2	3	4
5	6	7	8	9	10	11
12	13	14	15	16	17	18
19	20	21	22	23	24	25
26	27	28	29	30	31	

Meditations for the New Moon

I have found myself naturally gravitating over the last several years to using the dark moon as a solitary visioning time for the lunar cycle to come. I look forward to this time of the month—it has become a time to withdraw briefly from the world, go within and attune myself to the month ahead. There is incredible power in the imagination and I find that as I visualize more and more clearly what I am trying to achieve, amazing results follow.

I begin each new moon ceremony by carefully drawing the lunar cycle by hand in a big blank notebook I use for these visionings. I find that writing the 28 dates and the names of the weekdays by hand puts me in touch with time, giving me a true feel for how long 28 days really are. Then I let the spirit move me into meditation. May these twelve meditations serve as inspirations for your own new moon visionings. Blessed Be.

January

The first new moon in the year falls on January 20th, a Saturday. This lunar cycle has Brigit's Day, also known as Imbolg, the first cross quarter of the year. It is the traditional Celtic time of Initiation. Bride, the great Mother Goddess of the Celts, is the goddess of the flame, smithcraft, poetry. At this beginning of a new year, tune in to your creative spirit. What is it you wish to express more profoundly, more truly this year? Plan the steps this lunar cycle to begin something new, something you have wanted to do that you have never done before.

February

This new moon falls on Sunday, February 18. Take a real sabbath for yourself on this day of the sun. Unplug. Turn off the electricity. Light the candles.

This is the final lunar cycle of winter. It is the time to be designing your garden, the inner and the outer gardens. What seeds do you want to plant? Pay attention to your body, mind and spirit. Are you happy in your work and education? Are you at home in your body? Are you listening to your soul? Choose one activity for each week that will bring about more balance between the many aspects of your nature.

March

The new moon of March falls on Tuesday, the 19th. The Spring Equinox on the 21st is the major event of this lunar cycle—that amazing balance point between the light and the dark. We begin the waxing cycle of the year as the solar energy warms us up and the sap begins to flow. Celebrate, play. Find the wildflowers blooming. What makes you happy? Make this your new moon meditation. Then create the space in the next 28 days to spend more time doing what makes you happy. Bringing more joy into the world is one of the best things we can choose to do with our time here on Earth.

April

April's new moon is Wednesday, the 17th. Beltane on May 1 is the Night of the May Queen with the moon at its fullest May 3. Beltane, or May Day, is one of the great

Celtic fire ceremonies. It celebrates sexuality, love, passion. What lights your fire? What are you absolutely passionate about? Let these questions guide your new moon meditation and your visioning for this lunar cycle.

May

On this new moon, Friday, May 17th, look at what you have achieved. Honor yourself. Review. Read your thoughts and plans for the first 4 moons. Let yourself learn about your relationship to time. Do things take longer than you planned for? Do they happen more quickly? Are there surprises you hadn't anticipated? Let the wisdom that is blossoming from your meditations and visionings on the last 4 moons guide you as you vision this 5th lunar cycle.

June

This lunation carries us through the Summer Solstice on June 21st—the longest day of the year. It is the lunation with the most light of day available to us in the days on either side of solstice—maximum photons—a time to be outside. For this dark moon meditation, Saturday, June 15th, reflect on what aspect of your life you would like to enlighten or shed light upon.

July

New moon is Monday, July 15th. During this moon, we celebrate one of the cross quarters, Lammas, August 2, with the offering of first fruits to the Harvest Mother. What are your first fruits? The fruits of your seeds of imagination? Become aware of and honor your first harvest (it might be a new sense of time, or a flexibility of movement you have been seeking or the first draft of a manuscript or finally learning how to get online). On Lammas make an offering to the Harvest Mother in thanks.

August

The new moon of August is Wednesday, the 14th. This moon is the last full lunation of summer. In your visioning, remember summers of your childhood. What are your most vivid, favorite memories of summer days, summer nights? Have you spent as much time close to the earth as your body and heart long for? Bare feet on earth, swimming naked in mountain lake at sunrise are the soul's necessity. Create the time in this cycle of the moon to commune with Mother Earth more deeply than you ever have before.

September

The dark moon of this month falls on Thursday, September 12, and leads us to Autumn Equinox on September 21. This is the balance point, as we transit from summer to fall. Look back through the moons past to your first meditation of the year. Are you realizing your visions? Now is the time to bring the balance to those visionings you have not yet attended to. The cover of darkness will help you with these. Imagine good outcome in all your heartfelt endeavors.

October

This dark moon on Saturday, October 12, remember the witch, the healer, the woman of the grove, gatherer of herbs, seer of future time/dream time. This lunation celebrates the darkness with the great Celtic cross quarter of Halloween. To Hecate we bow and build the bonfire bright. Where in your life can you bring your witch to bear in ways that would be beneficial to your community? Do not be afraid to express the incredible healing power that dwells within you.

November

We're beginning to feel the pull of winter now. Are you going with the flow of the seasons or are you resisting the wane of the spiral year? For the new moon on Sunday, November 10th, imagine yourself a giant oak. When I was a child my aunt Sue had the largest Pin Oak in Ohio in her backyard. I spent a lot of time under that oak's great boughs. I imagine her in this meditation. Feel the natural ease of her letting go of her leaves, offerings to the earth for renewal. Let your imaginings guide you through this November moon.

December

The twelfth moon takes us through to a new year, the turning of the wheel, the 13th moon. These are the long nights that open us to a special kind of seeing. Appreciate and exercise your inner eye, often called the Third Eye, on this new moon, Tuesday, December 10th. Sit in total darkness. Let yourself go deep within—travel your infinite interior, raft the powerful rivers of your soul. See what you have never seen before. Before the high and holy festivals of the rebirth of light on Winter Solstice, December 21st, take time to love the dark mother night.

—*Claudia L'Amoreaux*

Key to Astrological Symbols

♈	Aries	♎	Libra	●	Dark Moon
♉	Taurus	♏	Scorpio	☽	First Quarter Moon
♊	Gemini	♐	Sagittarius	○	Full Moon
♋	Cancer	♑	Capricorn	☾	Last Quarter Moon
♌	Leo	♒	Aquarius	☉	Sun
♍	Virgo	♓	Pisces		

*All times are in Pacific Standard Time or Pacific Daylight Time.

Notes / Addresses

Notes / Addresses

Acknowledgments
All copyrights are held by the individual artists. Please do not reproduce without permission.

Text Credits

Anne Hillman—reprinted from *The Dancing Animal Woman: A Celebration of Life* ©1994 by Anne Hillman. Reprinted with permission of Bramble Books, Norfolk, Connecticut.

Clarissa Pinkola Estés—reprinted from *Creation Spirituality Magazine*, Summer, 1994 with permission.

Claudia L'Amoreaux—©1995 by Claudia L'Amoreaux from *The Book of Gaia*. Reprinted with permission of the author.

Diane Glancy—reprinted from *Looking for Home—Women Writing About Exile* ©1990 by Deborah Keenan and Roseann Lloyd. Reprinted with permission of Milkweed Editions, Minneapolis, Minnesota.

Ellen Evert Hopman—reprinted from *Tree Medicine, Tree Magic* ©1991 by Ellen Evert Hopman. Reprinted with permission of Phoenix Publishing, Custer, WA.

Elsa Gidlow—reprinted from *I Come With My Songs* ©1986 by Elsa Gidlow and Celeste West. Reprinted with permission of Booklegger Press, San Francisco.

E.M. Broner—©1995 by E.M. Broner. Reprinted with permission of the author from *Ceremonies to Go*.

Emily Brown—reprinted from *The Well of Living Waters* ©1977, published by The C.G. Jung Institute of Los Angeles. Reprinted with permission of the publisher.

Gladys A. Reichard—reprinted from *Spider Woman: A Story of Navajo Weavers and Chanters* ©1968. Reprinted with permission of The Rio Grande Press, Glorieta, NM.

Gwendolyn Endicott—reprinted from *Ancestors: Remembering the Elders* ©1994 by Gwendolyn Endicott with permission of the author. Published by Attic Press, Portland, Oregon.

Hue Walker—©1995 by Hue Walker. Reprinted with permission of the author.

Izumi Shikibu/Jane Hirshfield—reprinted from *The Ink Dark Moon: Love Poems by Ono no Komachi and Izumi Shikibu* ©1990. Reprinted with permission of Vintage Classics.

Jalaja Bonheim—reprinted from *The Serpent and the Wave: A Guide to Movement Meditation* ©1992 by Jalaja Bonheim. Reprinted with permission of Celestial Arts, P.O. Box 7123, Berkeley, CA, 94707.

Jane Caputi—reprinted from *Gossips, Gorgons and Crones* ©1993 by Jane Caputi. Reprinted with permission of Bear & Company, Inc., PO Box 2860, Santa Fe, NM 87504.

Jane Hirshfield—reprinted from *Women in Praise of the Sacred: 43 Centuries of Spiritual Poetry by Women* ©1994 by Jane Hirshfield. Reprinted with permission of HarperCollins Publishers, Inc., NY.

Jennifer Marie Murphy—reprinted from *The Beltane Papers* ©1994 by Jennifer Marie Murphy with permission of the author.

Karen Ethelsdattar & Ann Doemland—reprinted from *Liberating Liturgies* ©1989 by Women's Ordination Conference. Reprinted with permission of the author.

Louis Cunha—reprinted from *Liberating Liturgies* ©1989 by Women's Ordination Conference. Reprinted with permission of the author.

Louise Budde DeLaurentis—©1995. Reprinted with permission of the author.

Lucille Clifton—reprinted from *Quilting: Poems 1987–1990* ©1991 by Lucille Clifton. Reprinted with permission of BOA Editions, Ltd., Brockport, NY.

Luisah Teish—reprinted from *Carnival of the Spirit: Seasonal Celebrations & Rites of Passage* ©1994 by Luisah Teish. Reprinted with permission of HarperCollins Publishers, NY.

Maggie Howe—©1993 by Maggie Howe. Reprinted from *The Goddess Guild Gazette*, Summer 1993, with permission.

Marigold Fine—©1995 by Marigold Fine. Reprinted with permission of the author.

Marta Ayala—©1995 by Marta Ayala. Reprinted with permission of the author.

Melissa Harris—©1995 by Melissa Harris. Reprinted with permission of the author.

Merlin Stone—reprinted from *When God Was a Woman* ©1976 by Merlin Stone. Reprinted with permission of Doubleday, a division of Bantam Doubleday Dell Publishing Group.

Noel-Anne Brennan—reprinted from *Sagewoman Magazine* ©1994 with permission of the author.

Rachel Walberg—reprinted from *Jesus and the Freed Woman* ©1986 by Paulist Press. Reprinted with permission of the publisher.

Rose Romano—reprinted from *Sagewoman Magazine* ©1994 with permission of the author.

Rosie King-Smyth—©1995 by Rosie King-Smyth. Reprinted with permission of the author.

Rowena Pattee Kryder—reprinted from *Sacred Ground to Sacred Space* ©1994 by Rowena Pattee Kryder. Reprinted with permission of Bear & Company, PO Box 2860, Santa Fe, NM 87504.

Sappho/Mary Barnard—reprinted from *Sappho, A New Translation* ©1958 by The Regents of the University of California. Reprinted with permission of The University of California Press, Berkeley and Los Angeles, CA.

Susun S. Weed—reprinted from *Wise Woman Herbal: Healing Wise* ©1989 by Susun S. Weed. Published by Ash Tree Publishing, Woodstock, NY. Reprinted with permission of the author.

Shekhinah Mountainwater—©1995 by Shekhinah Mountainwater. Reprinted with permission of the author.

Every effort has been made to locate copyright owners and to secure permissions for material used in this calendar.

The Crossing Press
publishes many books of interest to women.
To receive our current catalog,
please call, toll-free
800-777-1048